Cook's Country

Spurn Head to St Abbs

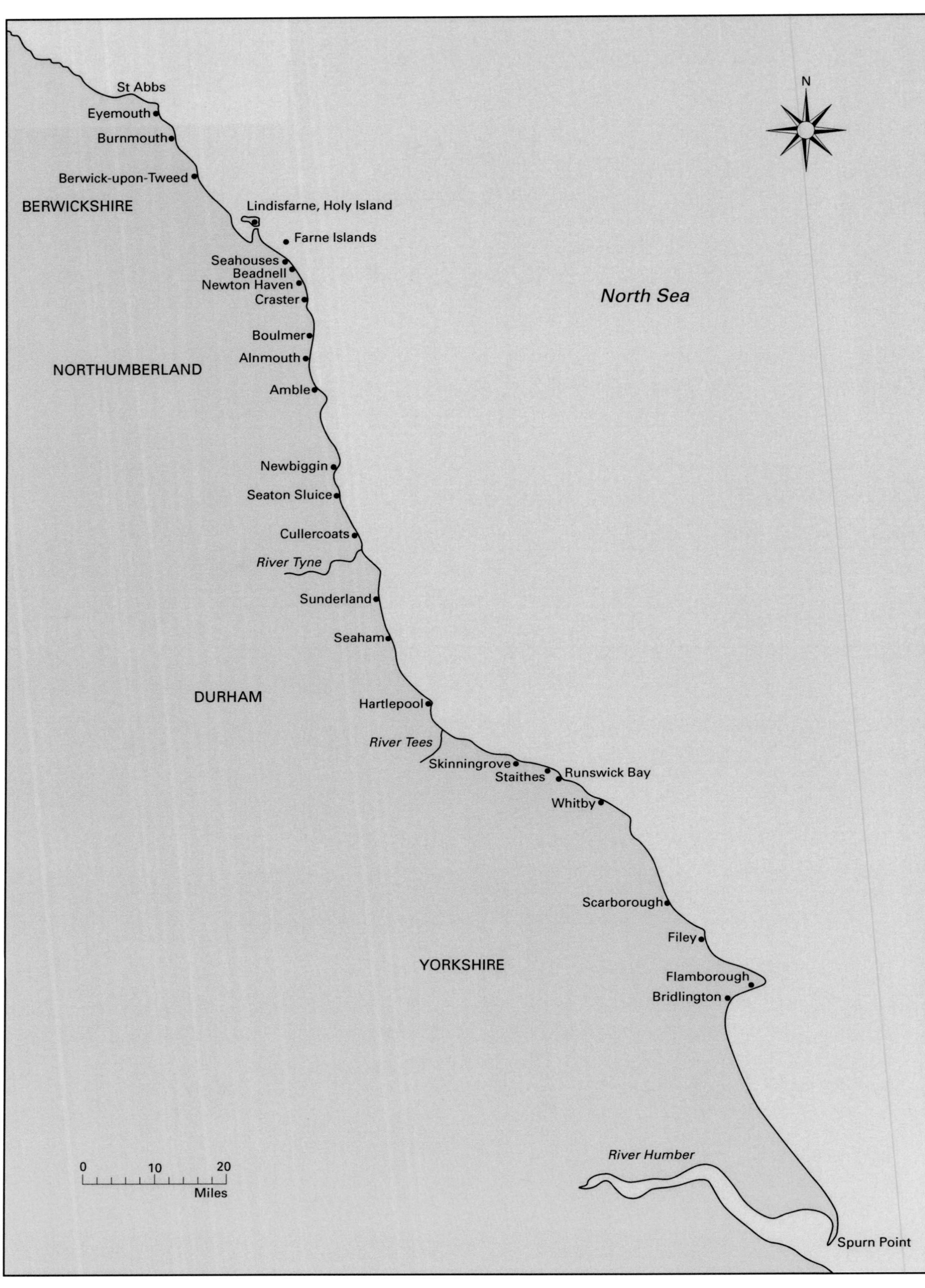

N
St Abbs
Eyemouth
Burnmouth
Berwick-upon-Tweed
BERWICKSHIRE
Lindisfarne, Holy Island
Farne Islands
Seahouses
Beadnell
Newton Haven
Craster
North Sea
Boulmer
Alnmouth
NORTHUMBERLAND
Amble
Newbiggin
Seaton Sluice
Cullercoats
River Tyne
Sunderland
Seaham
DURHAM
Hartlepool
River Tees
Skinningrove
Staithes
Runswick Bay
Whitby
Scarborough
Filey
YORKSHIRE
Flamborough
Bridlington
0
10
20
Miles
River Humber
Spurn Point

Cook's Country

Spurn Head to St Abbs

Henry Irving

Imray Laurie Norie & Wilson Ltd

Published by
Imray, Laurie, Norie & Wilson Ltd
Wych House, St Ives, Cambridgeshire PE27 5BT, England
✆ +44 (0)1480 462114
Fax +44 (0)1480 496109
Email ilnw@imray.com
www.imray.com
2016

First published in 2002 in Forth, Tyne, Dogger, Humber
First edition 2016

ISBN 978 184623 749 2

CAUTION
While every effort has been taken to ensure accuracy, neither the publishers nor the author will hold themselves responsible for errors, omissions or alterations in this publication. They will at all times be grateful to receive information which tends to the improvement of the work.

CORRECTIONAL SUPPLEMENTS
This pilot book will be amended at intervals by the issue of correctional supplements. These are published on the internet at our web site www.imray.com and may be downloaded free of charge. Printed copies are also available on request from the publishers at the above address.

THIS BOOK IS NOT TO BE USED FOR NAVIGATION
The plans in this guide are designed to support the text and should always be used together with navigational charts. They are not suitable for the plotting of positions from electronic navigation systems such as GPS. Even so, every effort has been made to locate harbour and anchorage plans adjacent to the relevant text.

The characteristics of lights may be changed during the life of the book, and that in any case notification of such changes is unlikely to be reported immediately.

All bearings are given from seaward and refer to true north. Scales may be taken from the scales of latitude. Symbols are based on those used by the British Admiralty – users are referred to *Symbols and Abbreviations (NP 5011).*

NOTICE
The UK Hydrographic Office (UKHO) and its licensors make no warranties or representations, express or implied, with respect to this book. The UKHO and its licensors have not verified the information within this book or quality assured it.

This work has been corrected to February 2016

Printed in the UK by Content Managed Communications Ltd

Contents

Preface

It is a rewarding and nostalgic experience to be asked to produce a pilot book for this magnificent stretch of the English coastline. My early childhood was spent at Billingham amidst the malodorous excrescences of ICI; later, my family moved to South Shields where, as a Sea Scout, I contemplated the wonders of Tyne Dock, the shipyards and Marsden Rock; my adolescence was articulated in Saltburn with a prospect on the one hand of the Redcar and Lackenby steelworks and on the other of Huntcliffe, Boulby and the glories of the north Yorkshire coast. My first job was in Hull, where I have lived ever since, and whilst the main focus of my sea sailing activity has been Norfolk, the Wash and the Humber, I have cruised the northeast coast to the Forth many times and I have attempted to poke my nose into all the harbours, large and small.

During the 1970s I made three such memorable cruises on Venture, my old Hull sailing shrimper, and the story of this cruising is recorded in a Yachting Monthly article of the day. I was greatly assisted in this activity by Guy Clephan's Sailing Directions. This worthy publication was revised and republished in 1990 by the late Rodney Mitchell, and to serve the increasing demands of the Northumberland sailors he increased its scope to stretch from the Humber to Rattray Head. Whilst this provided an invaluable cruising handbook it was felt that a pilot book with a more concentrated cruising focus would be appreciated. The Wash and Humber are dealt with in such detail in my *Tidal Havens* (Imray, 6th edition 2011). The Forth is similarly covered by Nicholas Thompson's *Pilot Handbook* (Forth Yacht Club) so it falls to me to deal with the coast of my childhood – Spurn to St Abbs. Since the last edition of Sailing Directions there has been a lot of major activity – marinas and barrages seem to spring up everywhere, utilising development grants and millennium money – so there is much to describe. The steady growth in popularity of yachting on the coast is to be applauded for it is rich with scenic and historic interest. The combination of natural beauty and manifest industrial history is probably unique on the English coast.

In preparing this volume I have made extensive use of oblique aerial photographs of almost all the harbours described. The bulk of these were supplied by Airfotos, Ltd. of Newcastle, though shots of Scarborough, Bridlington and Flamborough Head are courtesy of Richmond and Rigg of Hull. My own efforts at terrestrial photography were beefed up by contributions from my old friend Paul Cooper as he cruised the Audrey up and down the coasts of Yorkshire, Durham and Northumberland this summer, and from my brother Ed for some shots within reasonable access of his home on Teesside. To Polly, my wife, I am ever grateful for support and encouragement constantly proffered.

Preface to the Second Edition

To celebrate the twelve year long restoration of my Paull shrimper, *Venture*, my son Joe suggested that we revisit by sea the harbours described in *Cook's Country*. This could only be achieved by rekindling the forty year old cruising enthusiasm of my old sailing pals Dave Nisbet and Barry Speakman. We duly inspected most of the harbours. It is a fairly durable cruising ground but significant improvements have been made in the Yorkshire harbours. The greatest change is on the Durham coast where the mooring potential of Seaham's North Dock has finally been recognized by the creation of a marina. Photographs of the new developments are down to Ken Turnbull and my wife Polly. John Crow and his Tradeline team assisted stoutly in the vigorous sailing involved. To all these I am grateful for support.

Henry Irving
Hull 2016

Sketch chart conventions

Each of the havens described in this pilot is accompanied by one or two sketch maps, designed to assist the user in picking out features which are useful in negotiating entry. These sketches are not substitutes for charts. It is assumed that visitors unfamiliar with the cruising ground will be in possession of up-to-date editions of the appropriate large scale Admiralty or Imray charts. For hinterland features, there is no substitute for the various Ordnance Survey maps which cover the area. The sketches simply attempt to combine features of both at an appropriate scale, to suppress features considered unimportant to the processes of approach, entry and mooring, and to highlight those that are considered important.

Buoys, floats, light vessels and other marks with their nomenclature for shape, colour, sound and light, are represented in the mode of the Admiralty charts. Lights on jetties and piers are shown as circles with the appropriate labelling. Posts and withies, which feature prominently as navigational aids in many of the havens, are shown as single vertical lines, carrying a top mark when this is the case, and colour labelled in the usual fashion.

Features on land are selectively taken from the topographical maps. Not all features are shown, but with charts of such a large scale, most land features have a utility, either as conspicuous markers to assist approaches or as useful guides to land-based activities. Roads, ditches, bridges, trees and buildings are, therefore, in nearly all cases fully represented, and if any feature has an obvious utility such as a shop, railway station or public house, it is clearly labelled.

Recommended charts of the cruising ground

Admiralty

1190 Flamborough Head to Blakeney Point 1:150,000

1191 Tyne to Flamborough Head 1:200,000

1192 Saint Abb's Head to the River Tyne 1:200,000

121 Flamborough Head to Withernsea 1:75,000

129 Whitby to Flamborough Head 1:75,000

134 River Tees to Scarborough 1:75,000

152 River Tyne to River Tees 1:75,000

156 Farne Islands to The River Tyne 1:75,000

160 Saint Abb's Head to the Farne Islands 1:75,000

1188 River Humber - Spurn Head to Immingham

104 Approaches to the Humber Traffic Separation Scheme

1882 Bridlington and Filey

1612 Harbours and Anchorages on the East Coast of England and Scotland

2566 Tees and Hartlepool Bays

2567 Approaches to Tees Bay

1627 Harbours on the East Coast of England

1935 East Coast - Approaches to Blyth, River Tyne and Sunderland

1626 Blyth

1934 Entrance to the River Tyne

111 Berwick-Upon-Tweed to the Farne Islands

Associated British Ports

River Humber: Spurn Head to Barton Haven
River Humber: Barton Haven to Burton Stather

From ABP (Humber) Port House, Northern Gateway, Hull HU9 5PQ
✆ 01482 327171
www.humber.com

Imray, Laurie, Norie & Wilson

C24 Flamborough Head to Fife Ness 1:250 000 WGS 84

C29 Harwich to Whitby 1:285 000 WGS 84

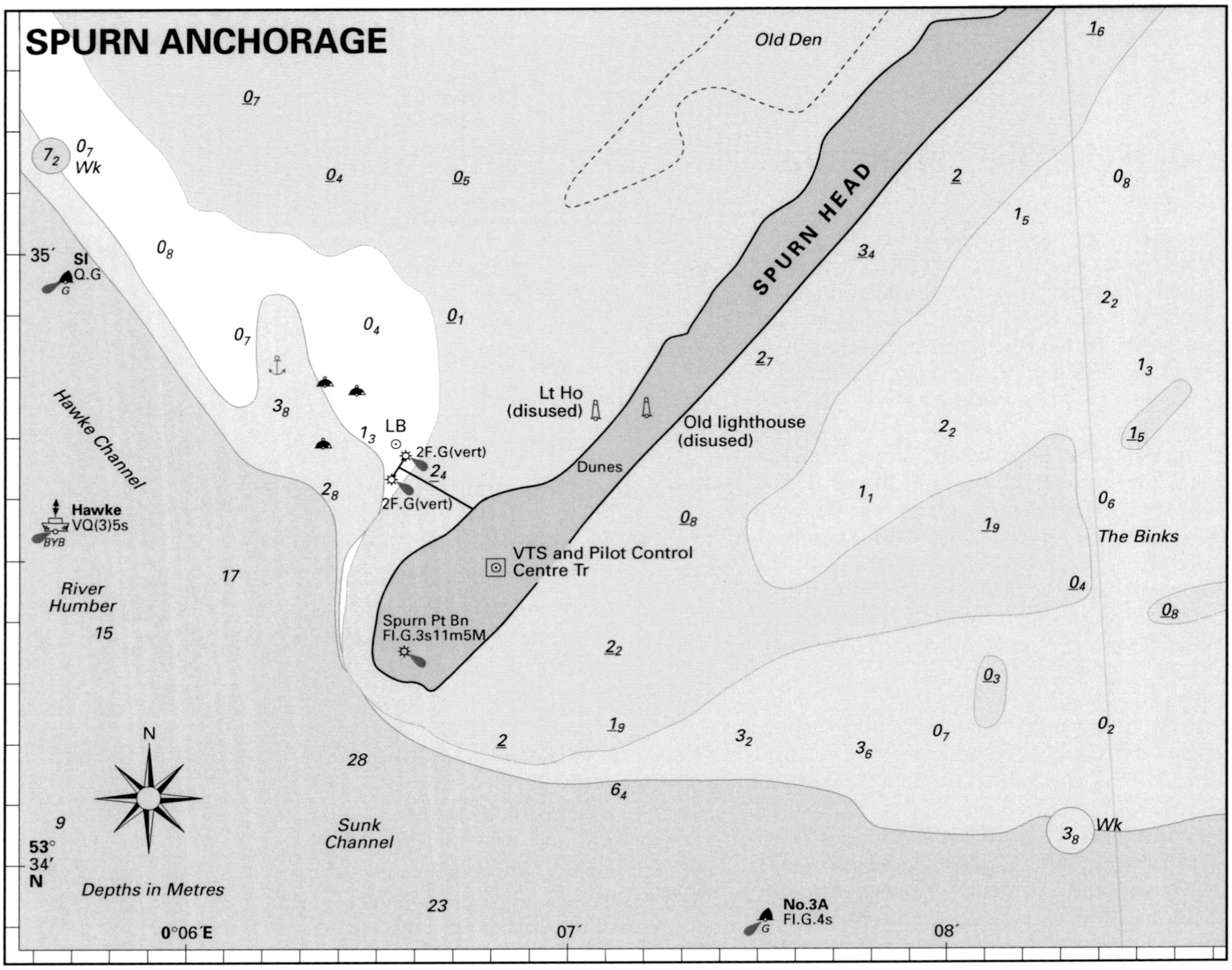

SPURN ANCHORAGE

Old Den
SPURN HEAD
35′ Sl Q.G
Hawke Channel
Hawke VQ(3)5s
BYB
River Humber
Lt Ho (disused)
Old lighthouse (disused)
LB
2F.G(vert)
2F.G(vert)
Dunes
VTS and Pilot Control Centre Tr
Spurn Pt Bn Fl.G.3s11m5M
The Binks
Wk
Sunk Channel
53° 34′ N
Depths in Metres
0°06′E
07′
08′
No.3A Fl.G.4s

Spurn Head *Richard and Rigg*

Southern approaches

The north east, as a cruising ground, can be characterised in terms of deep and rocky harbours, clear water, relatively weak tidal streams and a fascinating industrial history. As such it stands in striking contrast to its neighbouring cruising ground to the south – the tidal havens of the Humber and Wash. Here, the low sandy or marshy coasts, the big tidal range and the fast moving tidal streams all conspire to provide a different cocktail of challenge to the yachtsman. Swirling, silt-laden waters hide numerous sandbanks and the harbours are only accessible in the top half of the tide. To compensate for these difficulties the shoreside attractions have, in most cases, a rural flavour which can provide a great deal of pleasure and peace.

Between the two cruising grounds stands the Holderness coast – thirty miles of what must be ranked the most featureless stretch of coast in Britain, and one which is almost always regarded as a coast of passage. There are only a couple of things to point out to the passing visitor: Spurn anchorage and the anchorages on the Holderness coast.

Spurn

Although essentially part of another cruising ground of an altogether different flavour (Ref. *Tidal Havens*, Imray) I include Spurn in this volume because it is the only anchorage on this coast which gives shelter from winds from the north and east. The anchorage lies immediately west of the tip of the sandspit near to the Pilot jetty and the Humber Lifeboat moorings. There is quite a large area giving an ideal 3m depth at LWS and although the tidal stream around the very tip of the spit is fierce, there is virtually no flow in the anchorage. The transit of the two disused lighthouses is a useful guide to depths. North of the transit, a craft drawing 1·5m will take the ground at LWS. A strong breeze from SW to NW can make this anchorage uncomfortable but there are plenty of opportunities further north to cope in such circumstances.

A walk ashore has a rather gaunt interest. The Humber Lifeboat is the only one with a permanent crew because the remote location would make voluntary manning impractical. The small community of lifeboatmen and their families would make an interesting study for the community sociologist, but from the point of view of the visitor they represent the only chance of a lift if the comforts of the tavern at Kilnsea are sought. It is a 5 mile walk and although the Nature Reserve contains some fascinating flora and fauna, to do it twice would tax the resolve of even the most determined reveller.

The Holderness Coast

Immediately to the east of Spurn Point is an irregular shoal of sand and shingle known as the Binks. This is well indicated by the Humber entrance buoyage and should be avoided except near HW when it can be cautiously crossed. From here northwards to Bridlington the Holderness coast stretches unbroken – a 30 mile line of low boulder clay cliffs that are constantly being attacked and undermined by the sea. The current loss of land is on average 3m per year with the result that numerous historically recorded villages have disappeared and the development of coastal settlements has consequently not seemed a sensible proposition. Only at Withernsea and Hornsea has there been seaside development and the local authorities have to spend and struggle to fend off the erosion. Presumably, if the erosion process continues and the doughty inhabitants of those two towns maintain their spirited resistance, they will eventually become fortified peninsulas or even islands.

The coast is basically clean and the holding ground is good, so an anchorage can be made anywhere in offshore conditions. Armed with an OS map the intrepid yachtsman can scramble up the boulder clay cliffs and seek out interest and sustenance at a variety of villages, though only Hornsea and Withernsea present realistically convenient spots for revictualing and carousing.

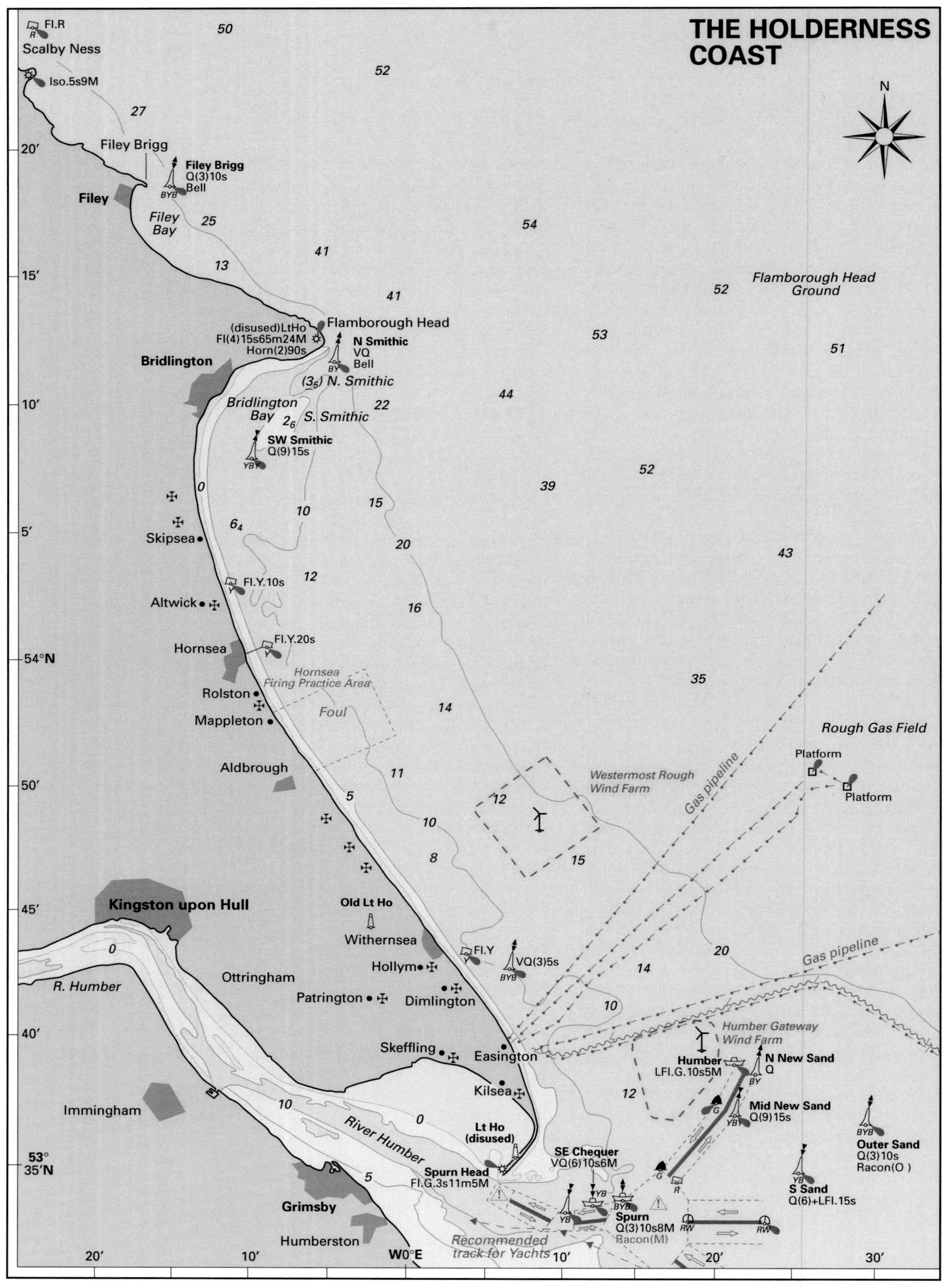
THE HOLDERNESS COAST
N
Fl.R
Scalby Ness
Iso.5s9M
Filey Brigg
Filey Brigg
Q(3)10s
Bell
Filey
Filey Bay
Flamborough Head
(disused)LtHo
Fl(4)15s65m24M
Horn(2)90s
N Smithic
VQ
Bell
N. Smithic
Bridlington
Bridlington Bay
S. Smithic
SW Smithic
Q(9)15s
Flamborough Head Ground
Skipsea
Fl.Y.10s
Altwick
Fl.Y.20s
Hornsea
Hornsea Firing Practice Area
Rolston
Foul
Mappleton
Aldbrough
Westermost Rough Wind Farm
Gas pipeline
Rough Gas Field
Platform
Platform
Kingston upon Hull
Old Lt Ho
Withernsea
Fl.Y
VQ(3)5s
Hollym
Ottringham
R. Humber
Patrington
Dimlington
Gas pipeline
Humber Gateway Wind Farm
Skeffling
Easington
Humber
LFl.G.10s5M
N New Sand
Q
Kilsea
Immingham
Mid New Sand
Q(9)15s
River Humber
Lt Ho (disused)
Outer Sand
Q(3)10s
Racon(O)
SE Chequer
VQ(6)10s6M
Spurn Head
Fl.G.3s11m5M
S Sand
Q(6)+LFl.15s
Grimsby
Spurn
Q(3)10s8M
Racon(M)
Humberston
Recommended track for Yachts
20′
15′
10′
5′
54°N
50′
45′
40′
53° 35′N
20′
10′
W0°E
10′
20′
30′

Bridlington

The massive protection offered by Flamborough Head against any kind of northerly storm or swell is a unique enough feature on England's North Sea coast to have long attracted the attention of seafarers. When to this is added the lesser, but still significant, protection from E and SE swells given by the Smithic Shoal, and the small river outlet afforded by the Gypsey Race then it is unsurprising that a harbour has long featured at this spot. The town and priory of Burlington was centred more than a mile inland but records indicate the long existence of a harbour at Bridlington Quay. In 1113 the ownership of the harbour was transferred from Gilbert de Gant to the Priory, and throughout mediaeval times wool was the principal export. Henry VIII took over the harbour after the Dissolution and embarked on a major rebuilding programme. With a typical touch of irony he ordered the timber frame piers to be infilled with stones from the destroyed Priory for strengthening purposes. For the next 300 years this harbour functioned, despite many breaches by the sea. Agricultural exports, coal imports and fishing were the mainstays, and shipbuilding flourished until the 19th century. From 1816 until 1848 John Rennie, the noted harbour engineer, was commissioned to rebuild and expand the port and by 1848 the stone-girt harbour that we see today was in place.

Commerce declined almost as soon as the new harbour was built, due largely to the arrival of the railway. As a consequence Bridlington was spared the jackboot of 19th century industrial port expansion and for the past 160 years an agreeable amalgam of tourism, pleasure boating, commercial fishing and pleasure angling has characterised the place. Passenger boat excursions to Flamborough and Bempton cliffs continue in summer to this day; commercial fish landings are down owing to the stringent fishing quotas in the North Sea but pleasure angling is catered for by the numerous cobles lying on the Chicken Run – the central harbour pier. Bridlington is often regarded as the third and most lowly of the trio of harbour gems on the Yorkshire coast and indeed its scenery is not quite so spectacular as Whitby and Scarborough. It offers, however, an agreeable mixture of history, architecture, maritime activity and jollity which will please the visitor.

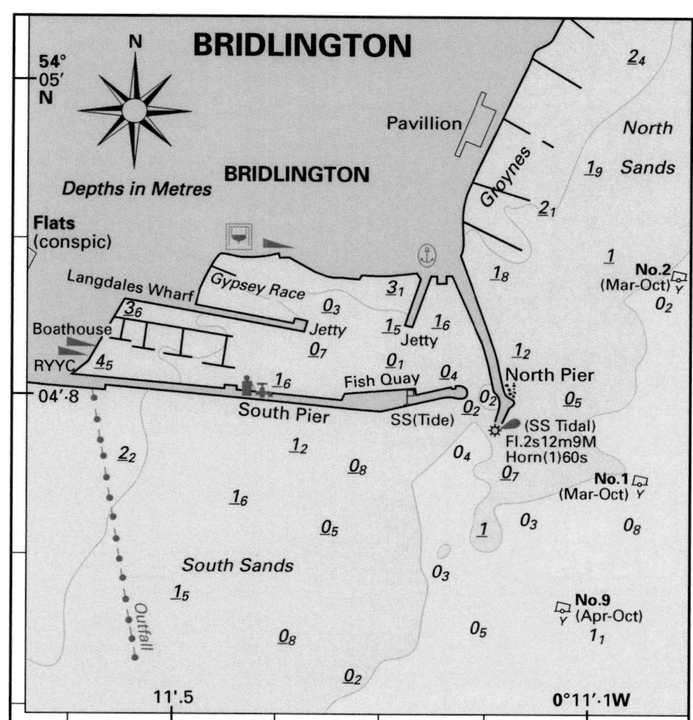

Approaches and entry

Bridlington Bay, to the south of Flamborough Head, is protected from winds from S through W to NE. The only circumstances in which approach and entry can be dangerous is strong weather from E and SE, when the off-lying Smithic Shoal gives breaking water and the harbour entry becomes untenable.

Bridlington entrance

Bridlington *Airphotos*

Approach to the pontoons

At the lowest of spring tides the harbour dries out completely. Indeed, even outside the harbour altogether is an unstable shoal called the Canch which sometimes dries. Most low tides, however, leave some water in the harbour entrance and on the neapest of tides a vessel drawing 1·5m can pass at low water, though it will not be possible to proceed far up the harbour. There is a tidal signal on the lighthouse at the end of the North Pier. Perversely, this shows red (flag by day, light by night) when there is more than 2·7m in the harbour entrance. When there is less water than this a green light is shown at night (no flag). A general guide for entry for a vessel drawing 1·5m is four hours either side of HW on springs ranging to full tide use on the most neap of tides.

Moorings

Bridlington is a Trust Harbour, run on non-profitable lines by a trust of 22 commissioners and administered on a day to day basis by the harbourmaster (✆ 01262 670148. VHF Ch12). The local pleasure craft, mainly belonging to members of the Royal Yorkshire Yacht Club, moor at the upper end of the S harbour branch, taking the bottom against pontoons provided by the harbour authority. Visitors will be allocated a vacant pontoon or a suitable place against the inner part of the South Pier. The bottom is of soft mud. The harbour dues are calculated on an area basis (LOA x beam) and in 2015 the normal rate for a visitor was £2.88 (+ VAT) per square metre per week, the daily rate being one seventh of this. A concessionary charge of £20.00 (incl. VAT) for any visiting vessel is available to cover a period of three calendar days provided:

- It is the first visit in any one year (1 April – 31 March)
- The stay is no more than three days
- Accounts are paid before departure.

Facilties

The co-existence of small fishing boats and local yachts has generated a lot in the way of harbour facilities. There is a travelhoist big enough to handle inshore trawlers; there are slipways, a scrubbing grid and a co-operative chandlery outlet. Standard marina services (water, electricity, security) are available and it is easy to fuel up. The RYYC clubhouse across the road from the neck of the S pier always provides a warm welcome, offering bar, showers and meals.

The town centre is immediately adjacent to the harbour on its northern side. Here are to be found banks, pubs, shops and cafés in abundance. The railway station, with trains to Hull and Scarborough, is less than half a mile inland and adjacent to it is a very large supermarket.

At the time of writing there is a controversial proposal to build a marina to the south of the harbour. The East Riding council are promoting the project, seemingly unaware of the proliferation of marina space elsewhere in the North East. Opposed to it are the harbour users and most of the population of Bridlington. Since it would virtually obliterate the present harbour, the south beach, the Spa and the view from dozens of elegant promenade properties, such opposition is unsurprising. The provision of better facilties for Bridlington's yachtsmen could easily be achieved within the confines of the existing harbour at a fraction of the cost. It is hoped that this project never gets off the ground for the essence of historic 'Brid' would be destroyed at a stroke.

Yorkshire coast anchorages

Flamborough

The chalk hills of the Yorkshire Wolds terminate spectacularly in Flamborough Head – an extremely large promontory which has certain interesting consequences for the mariner. On the one hand, on a coast which is characterised by fairly slight tidal streams, at Flamborough they are funnelled and concentrated to give a fierce stream that can exceed 3 knots at springs. It is necessary, therefore, when passage planning, to ensure a favourable stream around the Head. It must also be noted that irregularities of the seabed give rise to overfalls which, when aggravated by wind contrary to the tide, can be dangerous to small craft. In such circumstances it is best to keep at least 2 miles offshore.

A second consequence of the sheer size of Flamborough is that it gives two possibilities for anchorage that nicely complement each other. In winds from W round through N to NE, the South Landing can be used. In winds from SW round through S to SE, the North Landing is the one to opt for. Both are delightful spots with a wealth of bird life and both have good holding ground. Cobles work off the beaches at both places and the more diligent of the Flamborough fishermen

Flamborough
Richmond & Rigg

Flamborough Head from the S

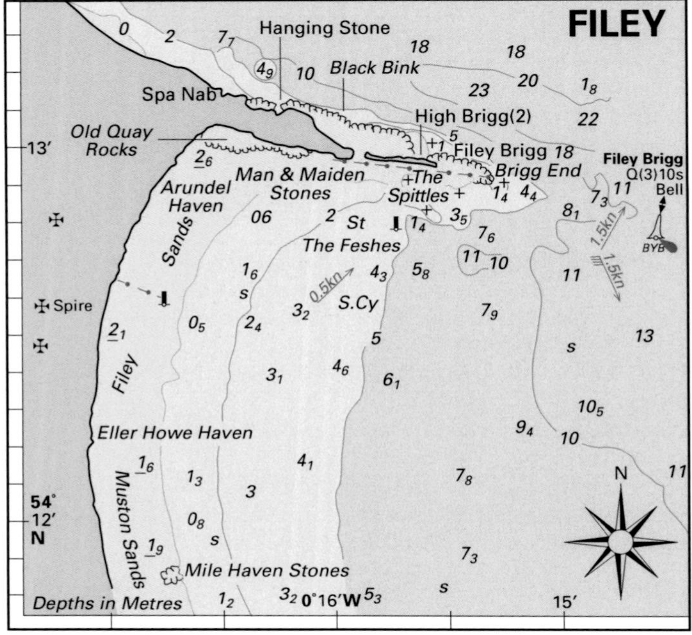

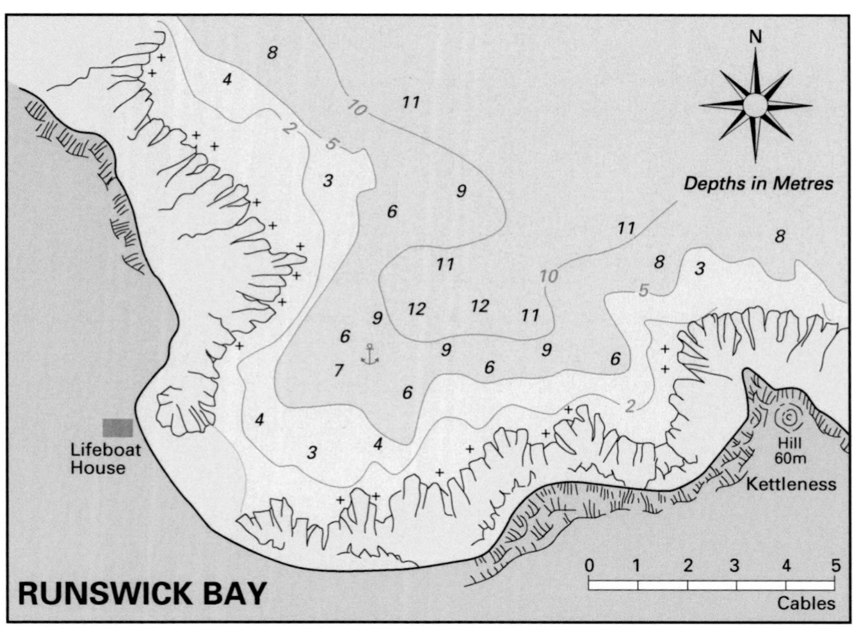

keep cobles at both spots to ensure better possibilities for working their pots. The village, a substantial one with many taverns and shops, is situated about halfway between – about a mile from each landing. In addition, the North Landing sports a couple of pub/restaurants which are very popular with birdwatchers and holiday makers in season.

Filey

Forever associated in the popular mind with Butlin's, it is often overlooked that Filey is an elegant and attractive little Victorian seaside town. Butlin's has long ceased to operate here, and although the surrounding area remains popular for caravan holidays the town itself is worth a visit and is rarely too crowded to be uncomfortable.

The Brigg is a natural rock breakwater which gives shelter from all offshore and northerly weather. There is good holding ground everywhere, and the best shelter can be found off the Coble Landing about halfway between the conspicuous 'ravine' and the base of the Brigg, which is, in addition, marked at its extremity by an E cardinal buoy.

Runswick Bay

North of Scarborough, the Jurassic geology of the North York Moors is the chief determinant of the wonderful and varied cliff scenery. Underlying sandstones, ironstones and shales weather differentially creating ravines and towering cliffs in a bewildering abundance. These rocks yielded minerals in the past: jet, much valued for jewellery (especially in vogue during Queen Victoria's 'black' phase); alum, used in tanning and dying; and, most important, ironstone which was a contributory factor in the development of Cleveland's iron industry. The coast is littered with evidence of former mineral workings such as shale waste heaps and ruined shipment jetties. Perhaps the safest place for the yachtsman to investigate these things is an anchorage at Runswick Bay, a beautiful indentation with good holding ground and shelter from winds NW by W to SSE. The bay is best entered on a heading of 225° and there is plenty of room to select a central anchorage in 3–7m. The east side of the bay shows evidence of waste from jet mining and a short coastal walk to the NW will lead to Port Mulgrave, a remote and now ruined purpose-built harbour for the export of iron ore to Teeside. The iron was mined by means of an adit tunnel by which the ore was hauled directly to the harbour side.

Runswick itself is now simply geared to tourism of the more refined type and there is a pub, shop and hotel/restaurant. This is indeed a pleasant spot to lie at anchor.

Skinningrove

Between the two highest cliff sections of the Yorkshire coast – Boulby with its slumped profile scarred by alum quarries and Huntcliff with its firm hard sandstone face – is the former iron centre of Skinningrove. Not only did it export ore from its hinterland of iron mines but it also imported coal to fuel its own blast furnaces. My childhood memories of the night skies of Saltburn being lit to the west at Hartlepool and Redcar and to the east at Skinningrove remain vivid.

Skinningrove has now lost its blast furnaces and merely retains some rolling mills but it still has the demeanour of a piece of County Durham dropped on the heritage coast of the North York Moors. Ashore are to be found pigeon lofts, allotments, working men's clubs and betting shops. As the maritime face of the Cleveland ironfield it is very interesting and rewarding if hardly pretty.

There is good holding ground on sand to the east of the stone ore jetty though the roughness of the jetty itself precludes an alongside mooring. Shelter is available for all offshore winds and the jetty prevents swell from working alongshore. The shoreside attractions are what might be expected of a place with Skinningrove's industrial history, but a thorough exploration of the valley right up to Carlin How can prove fascinating. The local pub, Timm's Coffee House, offers a warm welcome to the visitor and is a rich source of local lore.

Skinningrove
Capt J L Elliot

Skinningrove
Capt J L Elliot

Scarborough

The protection offered against northerly weather by Castle Rock, although fairly limited, is sufficient to have long encouraged harbour facilities in Scarborough. Prior to the mid-19th century this led to the growth of a community which, like Whitby, albeit on a smaller scale, was based on the building, owning and servicing of wooden vessels principally engaged in the Tyne coal and Baltic trades. Fishing was of solely local importance; indeed smaller places such as Filey, Runswick and Staithes were more important fishing stations than Scarborough or Whitby.

The coming of the railway in the mid-19th century had a profound effect on this hitherto isolated and remote coastline and it affected Scarborough in two striking ways. In the first place, the natural scenic beauty of the place attracted the well-heeled visitors typical of the days of early Victorian spa towns. Hotels, guest houses and bathing facilities sprang up and spectacular parks and other refined amenities were laid out. Today, the visitor from the sea can, if he narrows his gaze to erase some of the more garish amusement features of the promenade, still gain a good impression of the splendour of Victorian Scarborough.

The second impact of the railway was of direct concern to Scarborough harbour itself. The opportunity afforded in the marketing of fresh fish coincided with the arrival of large sailing trawlers from Brixham, Ramsgate and Lowestoft pressing ever northward in search of more fruitful fishing grounds. The Silver Pits and Dogger Bank teemed with sole, haddock and cod and the new arrivals looked to Scarborough as a convenient railhead landing port. Contemporary photographs show the harbour wall to wall with these huge smacks and the harbour was dredged and enlarged to accommodate them. By the 1870s smacks were being built in Scarborough and, in the days of sail, it prospered as the most northerly of the North Sea trawling stations.

But the days of sail were numbered. Experiments with steam engined trawlers in the 1870s in the northern ports of Shields, Sunderland and Hartlepool indicated the obvious advantages of the new technology.

Approaches to Scarborough

Scarborough *Ian Bracegirdle*

By the 1880s the whole trawling industry was turning over to steam and Scarborough was too far from essential coal supplies to be viable. The small scale of the harbour and the lack of engineering facilities also militated against it. As a result the fishing declined as spectacularly as it had arisen and by 1900 the smacks were gone. Fishing returned to Scarborough later in the 20th century with the development of near water motor trawlers but what the visitor sees today is but a rump of a once spectacular fishery boom.

Approaches and entry

Scarborough Castle, atop its Rock, is as conspicuous a landmark as an approaching mariner could wish for. From the north, Castle Rock must be cleared by 0·25 miles owing to the offlying rocks but in a big swell a much bigger offing will be necessary to avoid backwash. From the south the approach is clear with the exception of Ramsdale Scar 1·5 cables S of the harbour entrance. To avoid this it is necessary to remain E of the entrance until immediately prior to entry.

There are two harbours, each with separate entrances. The East Harbour dries, and entry can be effected with a vessel drawing 1·5m 3 hours each side of HW. This entrance can be closed by booms in heavy weather and for longer periods during the winter. In these circumstances entry must be made through the Old Harbour and behind the lighthouse, where there is a sliding footbridge. The Old Harbour has much more water. Indeed, a craft drawing 1·5m can enter at LWS in order to seek shelter and await sufficient water to move to the allocated berth. Care must be taken not to interfere with fishing boat and passenger boat movements in the Old Harbour. There are entry signals on the lighthouse: by day, a black ball is hoisted when there is at least 3·7m in the Old Harbour entrance; by night a white isophase light indicates the same. The depth in the entrance to the East Harbour is 1·5m less than this (i.e. 2·2m depth) so these signals are not really much use to the average yachtsman as an indicator of limits. If in any doubt the Port Control, manned 24/7, will advise (✆ 01723 373877). Strong winds from NE by E to SE create breaking seas in the approaches and make entry dangerous.

Moorings

The harbour is municipally owned and operated. Local boats have moorings all over the E harbour; those that can take the bottom easily do so on soft sand, those with keels are supported by wooden cradles.

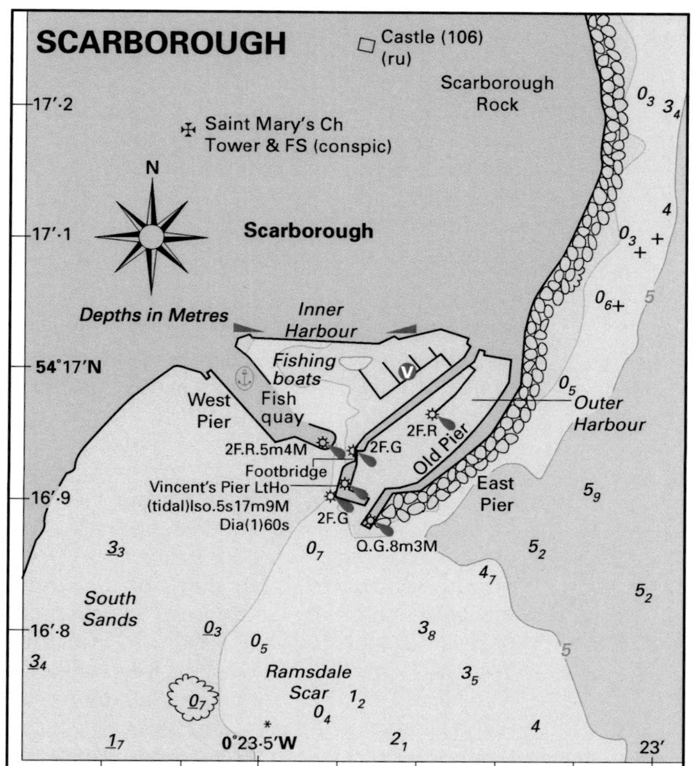

Scarborough entrances

Scarborough pontoons

Larger yachts tend to occupy the recently provided pontoon berths in the dredged eastern sector of the Old Harbour. Visitors will normally be allocated to a pontoon berth appropriate to their dimensions. Mooring fees for visitors in 2015 were £2.20 per metre per day (min. 8m) with a maximum stay of 14 days.

Facilities

Scarborough Yacht Club, in the lighthouse building, offers a welcome to visitors including the use of showers and bar. Water can be obtained on the quay nearby and fuel from the Fish Quay on the West Pier. Water, electricity and security are available on the pontoon berths, a key for which is obtainable from the Harbour Office (✆ 01723 373530) on the Fish Quay. As for town attractions, Scarborough has no peer, offering pubs, attractive shops of all kinds, theatres, cinemas, museums, spectacular parks and good rail connections to Hull and York. Dr Johnson's remarks may well be transferred to the context of the town, for when a man is tired of Scarborough he is tired of life; in Scarborough there is everything that life can afford.

Whitby *Airfotos*

Whitby

It is difficult to write of Whitby without indulging in a plethora of superlatives that might diminish each other. It drips with historical resonance and, what is more unusual, it shows. Its importance in the story of early Christianity is well documented – the Abbess Hilda, the dumb pig swain Caedmon who was suddenly gifted by God to produce poetry and song, the Synod of Whitby in the 7th century when the early Celtic church was finally embraced by the Church of Rome. All these are dramatically symbolised by the ruins of the abbey on the eastern cliffs.

It has been a bustling port for over 1000 years, reaching an apogee perhaps in the late 18th and early 19th centuries when it was a centre of shipbuilding and whaling. Captain Cook began his illustrious sea career here when he was bound apprentice to John Walker, ship owner and coal shipper, in 1746. He served his time in collier brigs, principally engaged in the coal trade between the Tyne and London, and by 1757 he was a master. At this point, however, he decided to join the Navy and the rest is a well-told story. The port of Whitby, however, flourished without him and there grew a vast whaling industry in which the famous Scoresby family loomed large. The bustling scene at Whitby in the early 19th century is tantalising to the imagination.

It is a pity that the port had gone somewhat into decline by the late 19th century, for we are left with a unique photographic record of that period from the remarkable photographer Frank Meadow Sutcliffe. His superb sepia shots of fishermen at work, children at play and ships in the harbour adorn the walls of pubs and the windows of galleries throughout the town and greatly assist the imagination in historical reconstruction. Yet the little town itself still gives assistance here. The streetscapes and roofscapes are still much as they were in Sutcliffe's day and a stroll around the streets and alleys of old Whitby is as delightful an experience as a cruising yachtsman could ever have.

Approaches

Whitby Harbour is essentially the lower reaches of the River Esk and the deep cleft formed by the river in the surrounding hills is a conspicuous feature. Additional confirmation is had from the prominent remains of the ruined abbey on the cliff top to the east of the harbour.

An approach from the north and north west presents no problems, but a vessel coming from the east must round Whitby

Approaching Whitby

Rock, a dangerous bush extending seawards from the Abbey cliffs. An eponymous N cardinal buoy marks the seaward extent of Whitby Rock. At the Rock Buoy the tide begins to flow SE some two hours after local LW and NW two hours after HW. This tidal flow must be considered when approaching the harbour, especially the considerable eastward set over the HW period.

The approaches are dangerous in heavy onshore weather and in such circumstances the Tees is a safer option.

Entry

The chart indicates a maintained depth of 0·7m at LAT. In fact this means that a vessel drawing 1·5m can enter the harbour and reach the Fish Quay at LWS providing the leading marks are strictly followed.

The entry leading marks are sited on the eastern side of the harbour slightly to the right of the tower of St Mary's church. The lower mark is a yellow triangle on a beacon, the upper a yellow circle with a black vertical line on the side of a house. The bearing from sea on these marks is 169°. This course should be held through both sets of piers until two similar marks on the E pier come into line astern. These marks carry fixed amber lights and give a back bearing of 029° right up to the Fish Quay, where temporary mooring may be obtained. Instruction can be obtained from the nearby Harbour Office (✆ 01947 602354) or from Whitby Harbour Radio VHF Ch11.

Moorings

Whitby Marina, the most suitable destination for visiting craft, is situated in the Upper Harbour beyond the swing bridge. The bridge opens on request each half hour for 2 hours either side of HW.

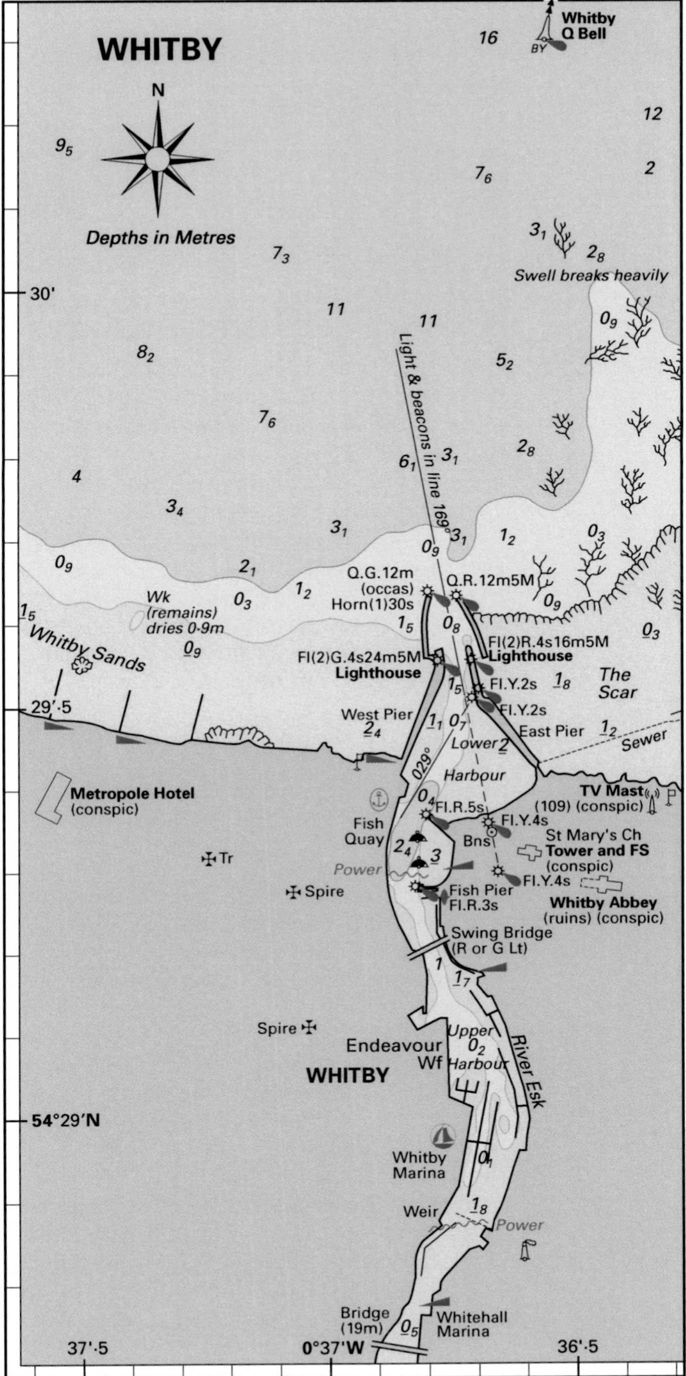

Vessels can call the bridge direct on VHF Ch 11 to request an opening. If arrival is outside bridge opening times then vessels will have to remain on the Fish Quay, taking care that the craft is constantly manned to facilitate the movement of fishing boats. There is a small waiting berth at the end of the Fish Pier on the east side which gives access to the shore.

The Marina (✆ 01947 600165) is a local authority operated facility and has pontoon berths on both sides of the river. Most are

Entering Whitby harbour
Isabel Eaton

permanently rented and the visitor must moor at the northern end of the pontoon on the west side above the cargo wharf. Visitors are allocated one of the first four berths on each side of the pontoon. There is a minimum depth of 2m and marina facilities are situated at the head of the gangway. Mooring charges for visitors in 2015 were £2.22 (+VAT) per metre per day, which includes the harbour dues and the marina mooring fees, minimum charge £17.80 (+VAT).

Facilities

Electricity and water are laid on to the marina pontoons but there is no fuelling berth. Fuel can be obtained from Eves Garage on New Quay Rd, near the swing bridge. The Marina Office block has shower and laundry facilities, and a chandlery is adjacent.

Across the road and in the direction of the railway station is a large supermarket. Immediately beyond this is the bustling town centre with shops and pubs (27 in all) to satisfy even the most demanding visitor.

Whitby sits surrounded by the North York Moors National Park and is undoubtedly the best base from which to explore this extremely picturesque area. The train and bus stations are adjacent to each other and it is relatively easy to plan circular day trips by combining train and bus journeys. If the visitor is exhausted by days at sea, however, there is sufficient in this wondrous little town to entertain for days. Even Dracula had a jolly time in Whitby.

Whitby marina

Staithes

Staithes has long been hostage to the sea. The impertinence of man trying to get a footing on this narrow ravine between two brooding cliffs is continually avenged by lumps of the place being snatched away by the savage waves. Captain Cook served as assistant to a haberdasher here from 1744 to 1746. It is surprising that he was not put off by some of the seas he must have seen. Certainly the shop in which he worked has long been devoured by such seas. A series of evocative pictures in the Cod and Lobster on the harbour front shows the waves dealing destruction to the pub on three or four occasions throughout the 20th century.

Originally fishermen relied on natural rock protection and the sanctuary offered by the mouth of the Roxby Beck at the higher stages of the tide, but the opportunities for iron ore shipment in the early 19th century resulted in the construction of breakwaters and wagonways. A small town of substantial three storey houses enlarged the original village of fishermen's cottages and services followed. From 1840, new technology enabled the working of larger seams at neighbouring Port Mulgrave and Skinningrove where blast furnaces were constructed so Staithes became fossilized in an early industrial form. As a consequence it is a delightful amalgam of architectural types – more substantial than the fishing village at Runswick but less austerely industrialised than its neighbour to the west at Skinningrove. The result is a charming little harbour which firmly merits a visit when offshore or quiet conditions prevail.

Approaches and Entry

The village does not become visible to the coastal cruising yachtsman until almost abeam, though the position can be identified relative to the conspicuous chimneys of Boulby potash mine inland and to the west. Once visible, a bearing of 225° straight into the harbour entrance will give the best water.

Entry may be made with a vessel drawing 1·5m from 3½ hours before HW until 3½ after, though it must be emphasised that in any kind of swell working onshore, the harbour is best avoided.

Mooring

The local cobles take the beach between the breakwaters in settled weather but retreat up the Roxby Beck to their winter moorings when there is onshore weather. Shoal draught or bilge keel craft can emulate this, but it must be noted that there is a footbridge across the beck a short distance above the LB house.

The only really feasible berth for visiting craft of a more substantial size is against the N pier in the angled section where there is a well-found wall ladder. There is a large boulder to the seaward end of the mooring which must be avoided but is clearly visible. Vessels drawing 1·5m will dry out here at LWS so a mast rope precaution is wise. At neaps such a draught may just about float all the time.

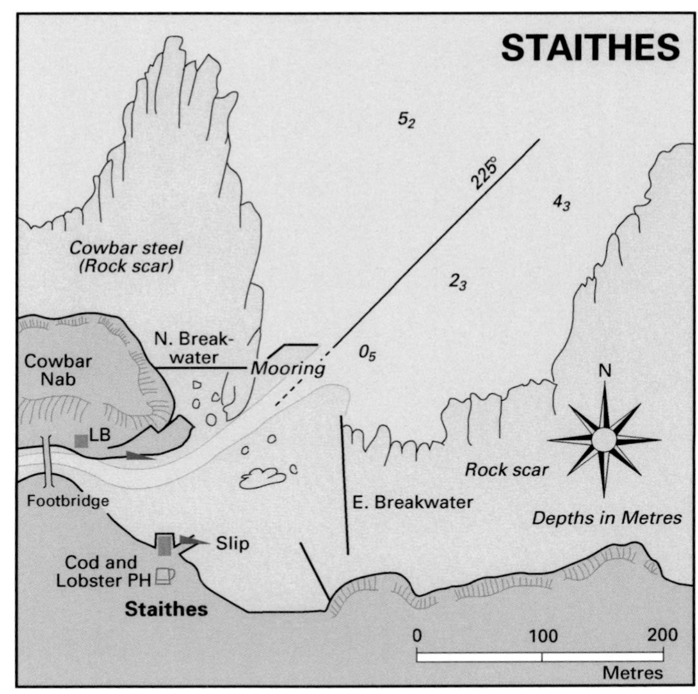

Staithes moorings

Staithes harbour *Isabel Eaton*

Staithes. The N breakwater has since been strengthened
Airfotos

Facilities

Basic quayside utilities are totally lacking. Indeed, at HWS it is not possible to pass from the N pier to the village without wetting the feet, but the delights of Staithes more than compensate. There are three lively pubs in the harbour section of the village, all of which provide meals and two of which provide bed and breakfast. There is also a butcher, a seasonal Italian restaurant and a PO/general store. Up the hill near the site of the old railway viaduct is another pub with frequent live jazz. A lateshop mini-market nearby can provide a full range of food, wine and cashback. The cruising yachtsman really must visit Staithes.

River Tees

It has long been the practice of pilot compilers and yachting writers to talk down the Tees or even completely ignore it. Heavy industrialisation, water and air pollution, lack of facilities, nothing to interest the visitor, heavy commercial traffic – all these have been cited as reasons for discouragement. It has to be said that it is all true, but there is a very important reason why the Tees should not be ignored. Between the two great estuaries at either end of this cruising ground – the Forth and the Humber – there is only one place that could be remotely described as estuarial, and that is the Tees. When to this is added the fact that it is situated almost exactly halfway, then its strategic utility becomes apparent, In certain weather conditions – gales from the NE and E – all the harbours described in this volume become dangerous or impossible. At night the dangers are even worse. In such conditions – and even with the highest levels of skill and prudence a sailor can be caught out – the Tees plays a vital role. Conditions in the approaches will not be pleasant in such circumstances but the entrance is infinitely safer than anywhere else. For this reason it merits description.

In addition, the recent opening of the Tees Barrage at Stockton has opened up a dozen miles of interesting tide-free cruising for those with suitable boats. It is easy to write off industrial places and press on in search of rural idyll, but, for many, industrial history is equally fascinating. When presented in a user-friendly and sympathetic fashion, as the Teesside Development Corporation have successfully done, then the attractions will be a lure to many.

Cowbar, Staithes
Isabel Eaton

From medieval times until the 19th century, Yarm was the lowest bridging point on the Tees and a port developed there. There is still evidence in this delightful little market town of quaysides and former industrial establishments nurtured by the presence of navigable water. The increase in size of shipping and the tortuous and time consuming tidal journey, however, led in early modern times to the rise of Stockton, farther downstream. In the 18th century Stockton was a bustling market town with substantial quaysides and shipping-related industries. With the arrival of the Industrial Revolution, the availability of coal in the hinterland and the possibility of raw material assembly by sea led to an explosion of industrial activity in Stockton, including coal export, iron making, shipbuilding and a myriad associated trades. The demand for better coal export facilities by the coal owners of SW Durham led to the construction of the Stockton and Darlington railway – a major first, and a massive improvement over the primitive horse-drawn wagonways that preceded it. Coal drops were built, a new bridge was built across the river and Stockton assumed Yarm's title of lowest bridging point, denying access to Yarm to masted vessels.

Yet the coal owners and ironmasters could not be satisfied. In the way of Yarm before it, Stockton was beset with problems of site congestion, distance and river shoals. By the mid 19th century new coal drops were being planned at 'greenfield' sites farther downstream at Middlesbrough on the S bank and Port Clarence on the N. The great ironmasters Bolckow and Vaughan built vast furnaces at Middlesbrough and a new town was rapidly established. Iron and steel making crept downstream in the late 19th century, finally reaching Redcar at the river mouth. In the 20th century any remaining green fields, though in truth they were already brown, were occupied by the huge chemical complex of ICI on both sides of the river at Billingham and Wilton. When no fields were left, the estuarial marshes were drained and infilled and yet more industry followed – petrochemicals and oil refining being the late 20th century vogue. Here, without a shadow of doubt, has developed the heaviest concentration of large scale industry in Britain.

Approaches and entry

The Tees is 'designed' to accommodate 'panamax' size vessels and the huge bulk carriers and tankers that use the port are not ultra-manoeuvrable. Accordingly the approaches and entry are staggeringly straightforward for the small boat owner. From the Tees Fairway RW pillar buoy a simple, dead straight, laterally-buoyed channel leads between the breakwaters known as the N and S Gare. Indeed, they are not so much breakwaters as devices to stop the longshore migration of sand, so the entrance is much more estuarial than the heavily-defended river mouths of Tyne and Wear. At night, fixed red leading lights lead from the Fairway Buoy on 210°. Once inside, buoyed channels lead towards various terminals in addition to the main route upriver. Because of the heavy commercial traffic it is essential to contact the Harbourmaster's Office (✆ 01642 452541, VHF Ch 14, callsign *Tees Harbour. Radio*) to declare intentions and to receive shipping movement advice.

Moorings

It remains true that there are few attractive moorings on the lower Tees. There are some mooring buoys, and space to anchor, on the SE shore directly inside the entrance at Paddy's Hole. Craft drawing 2m can lie afloat here, and members of the local South Gare Marine Club (✆ 01642 491039) will advise as to the best spot. Three sheltered drying basins, Paddy's Hole, Guy's Hole and Sand Hole provide a home for dozens of

Paddy's Hole, boat or shed?

Fisher community at South Gare

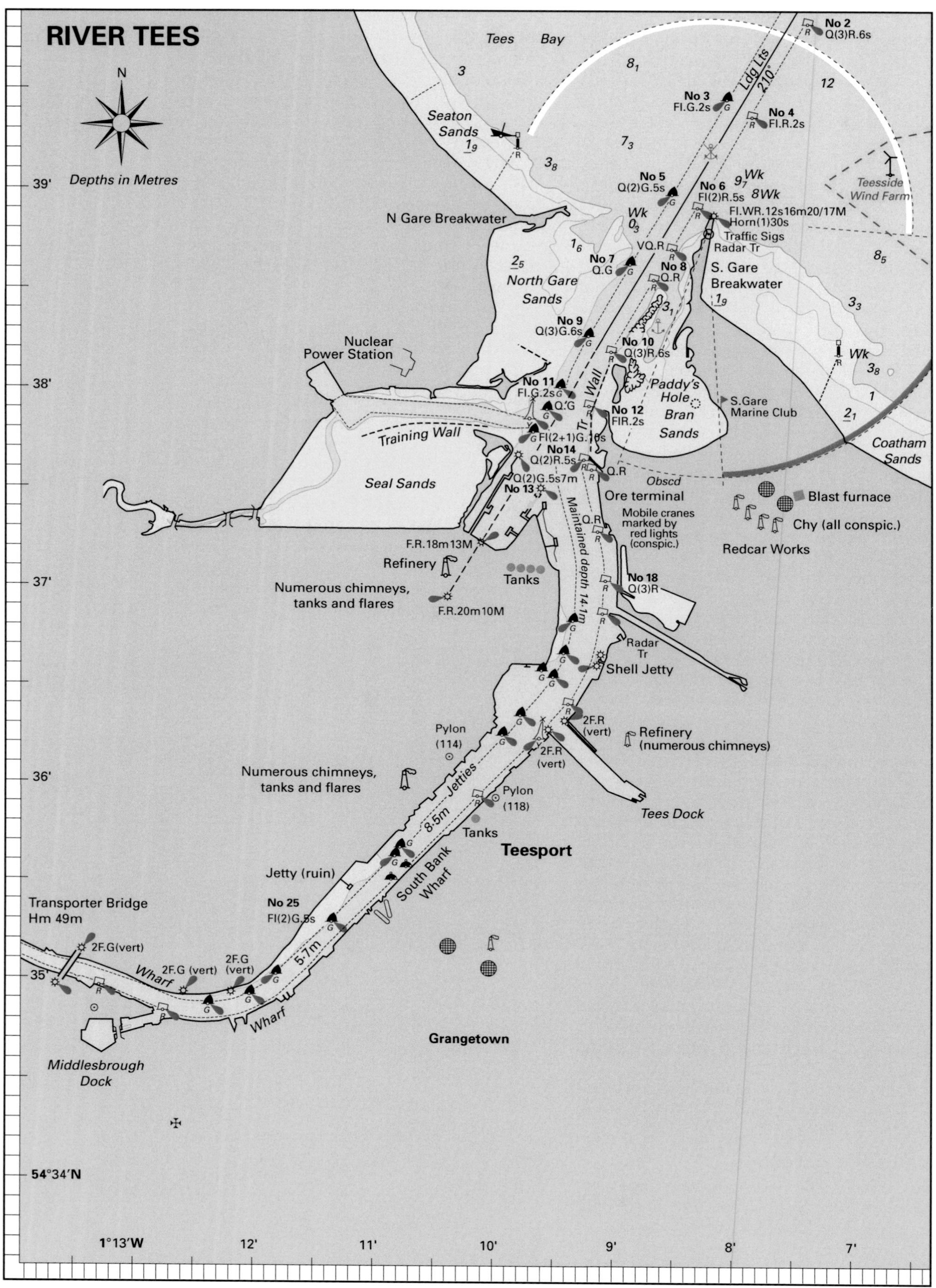
RIVER TEES
Depths in Metres
Tees Bay
Seaton Sands
N Gare Breakwater
North Gare Sands
Nuclear Power Station
Training Wall
Seal Sands
S. Gare Breakwater
Paddy's Hole
Bran Sands
S.Gare Marine Club
Coatham Sands
Teesside Wind Farm
Ldg Lts 210°
No 2 Q(3)R.6s
No 3 Fl.G.2s
No 4 Fl.R.2s
No 5 Q(2)G.5s
No 6 Fl(2)R.5s
Fl.WR.12s16m20/17M
Horn(1)30s
Traffic Sigs
Radar Tr
No 7 Q.G
No 8 Q.R
VQ.R
No 9 Q(3)G.6s
No 10 Q(3)R.6s
No 11 Fl.G.2s
Q.G
Fl(2+1)G.10s
No 12 FlR.2s
No14 Q(2)R.5s
Q.R
Q(2)G.5s7m
No 13
Obscd
Ore terminal
Mobile cranes marked by red lights (conspic.)
Blast furnace
Chy (all conspic.)
Redcar Works
F.R.18m13M
Refinery
Numerous chimneys, tanks and flares
F.R.20m10M
Tanks
Maintained depth 14.1m
No 18 Q(3)R
Radar Tr
Shell Jetty
2F.R (vert)
Refinery (numerous chimneys)
Pylon (114)
Pylon (118)
Jetties
8.5m
Tees Dock
Tanks
Teesport
Jetty (ruin)
South Bank Wharf
No 25 Fl(2)G.5s
5.7m
Transporter Bridge Hm 49m
2F.G(vert)
2F.G (vert)
2F.G (vert)
Wharf
Wharf
Middlesbrough Dock
Grangetown
54°34'N
35'
36'
37'
38'
39'
1°13'W
12'
11'
10'
9'
8'
7'

small fishing boats but they are so congested with moorings, slipways and sheds that any visitor must first anchor outside and seek local advice if he requires shelter or assistance here.

In Middlesbrough itself there are some ambitious improvements taking place in the Dock which is destined to become a water-fronted residential and amenity area. A half-height dock gate is planned so that an area of water is retained for visual amenity. The approaches to the gate offer mooring possibilities and substantial wall ladders close to town facilities. Another possibility is a quay berth on the Middlesbrough bank just upstream of the Transporter Bridge, though dirty wall ladders and a considerable rise and fall of tide will discourage all but the most determined town centre fanatic.

Farther upstream is the Newport Bridge, formerly lifting but now fixed in the low position at 6·4m MHWS, so craft with larger air draught cannot proceed to the delights that lie beyond. For those without masts or with sufficiently small ones, a whole new world of cruising possibilities has been opened up by the construction of the Tees Barrage. This holds the level of the Tees above it at a constant, average high tide level, excluding the polluted tidewater of the Lower Tees and creating an eleven mile stretch of clean water that comes fresh from the N. Pennine dales. This gives a variety of mooring possibilities both urban and rural. So recent is the development that not all the access plans are yet in place, but pleasant moorings can be had at Castlegate Quay in Stockton and at Yarm downstream of the bridge. Maximum dimensions for using the Barrage Lock are 25m x 6m and craft drawing up to 2·5m can navigate the river as far as Yarm. Beyond Yarm the depth gradually reduces to 2m at Low Worsall. Possibilities above this depend on the amount of fresh in the river. The maximum air draught is 5·5m The non-tidal section is run by the Canal and River Trust (✆ 01642 633773) and the daily registration charges in 2015 were: 1–5m, £9.70; 5–7m, £12.00; and 7–10m, £13.00. These fees include VAT and allow the use of the Barrage Lock without any further payment.

Facilities

The type of facility normally sought by the cruising yachtsman is not easily available on the tidal Tees. The S Gare Marine Club at Paddy's Hole has a bar but it is 3·5 mile walk to more comprehensive facilities in Redcar. The proximity of Hartlepool across the bay would normally divert attention from such a lonely spot.

Middlesbrough Transporter Bridge

The Tees Barrage

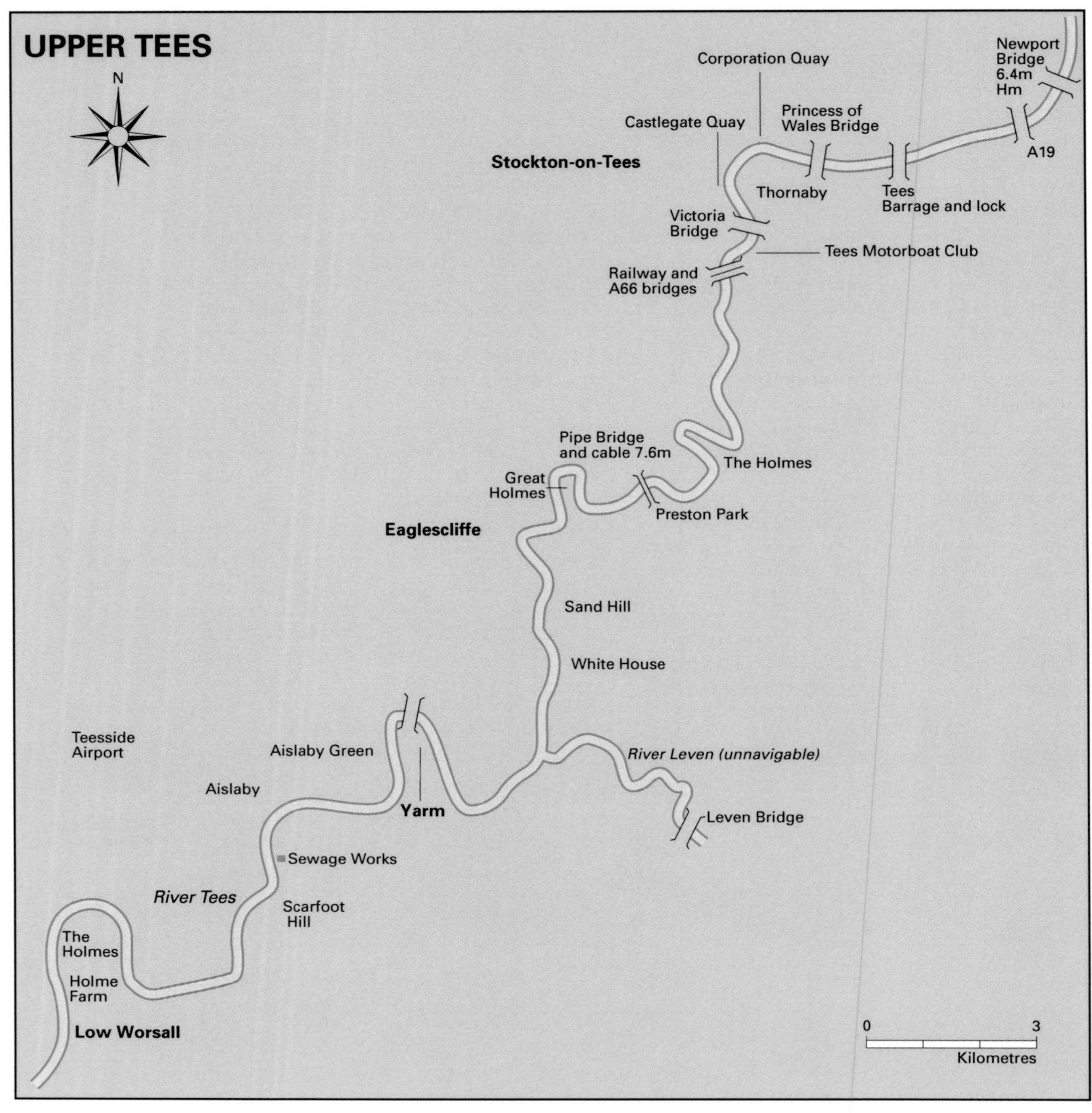

Middlesbrough town centre, of course, offers all the services typical of a large town and it is remarkably close to the proposed developments in the Dock. The swirl of urban motorways makes the place less than attractive to the visitor, but the facilities are there, and close at hand.

A mooring at the Transporter might appeal to the student of the seedier side of cities. In the area of town known as 'over the border' there are some lively and interesting pubs and clubs which will serve to entertain the visitor of a rumbustious disposition, though this is not to be recommended for a cosy family treat.

The 'new waters' above the Barrage lead peacefully to a plethora of facilties. The attractive High St of Stockton offers shops, pubs and entertainment a short hop from the newly-refurbished quays. Yarm beckons the visitor further with plenty more of the same, albeit at a more cosy scale. Railway stations are handy at Yarm, Thornaby and Middlesbrough, permitting crew change. A sojourn on the non-tidal Tees can be a very pleasant and relaxing alternative to the rigours of the sea.

Hartlepool

Hartlepool Heugh, or the Headland as it is locally known, has been valued for centuries by mariners for the natural harbour it creates. St Hilda's church dates from the 12th century and was built on the site of a 7th century Saxon monastery. Trade and industry flourished from mediaeval times and an important fishery developed. During the Napoleonic Wars, on a stormy December night, a French privateer got into difficulties on the nearby rocks and foundered. Some days later, among the wreckage washed ashore, local fishermen found a bedraggled, chattering monkey dressed in a military uniform. The admirably patriotic fishermen held a court martial, deemed the monkey to be a French spy and administered the appropriate penalty by stringing the creature up on the halyards of a coble on the beach. Since that date there has been no recorded incidence of Hartlepudlian aggression towards visitors, maritime or otherwise, but if a cruising yachtsman feels his appearance to be at all simian, then caution would be prudent.

The mid-19th century witnessed an explosion in demand for port facilities. South West Durham coal required export outlets, and the advantages of raw material assembly led to the growth of iron and steel making on a massive scale on open land to the south of the Headland. An enormous Victorian dock complex was constructed and a new town was built to accommodate workers and traders. This was known as West Hartlepool and its neo-classical architecture reflected the prosperity and aspirations of its citizens. Coal export, timber import and steel were the solid basis of this prosperity.

The Depression of the 1930s hit Hartlepool's economy very hard, and although some postwar recovery took place, the basic industries were found to be in terminal decline – a decline which no amount of government assistance seemed able to halt. The docks, and to some extent the town itself, became a watchword for industrial and urban decay and dereliction. A visit to Hartlepool in the 1970s and 80s was a saddening and chastening experience.

The urban and maritime revival of the 1990s stands, therefore, as an impressive testimony to the potency of thoughtfully applied development finance. The Hartlepool of today is a joy to visit. The scaled down docks are flourishing, with lock-free wharfage in Victoria Harbour dredged to 9m LAT catering for bulk and general cargo. RoRo berths in the North Basin cater for car imports, timber and

Hartlepool marina and historic quay

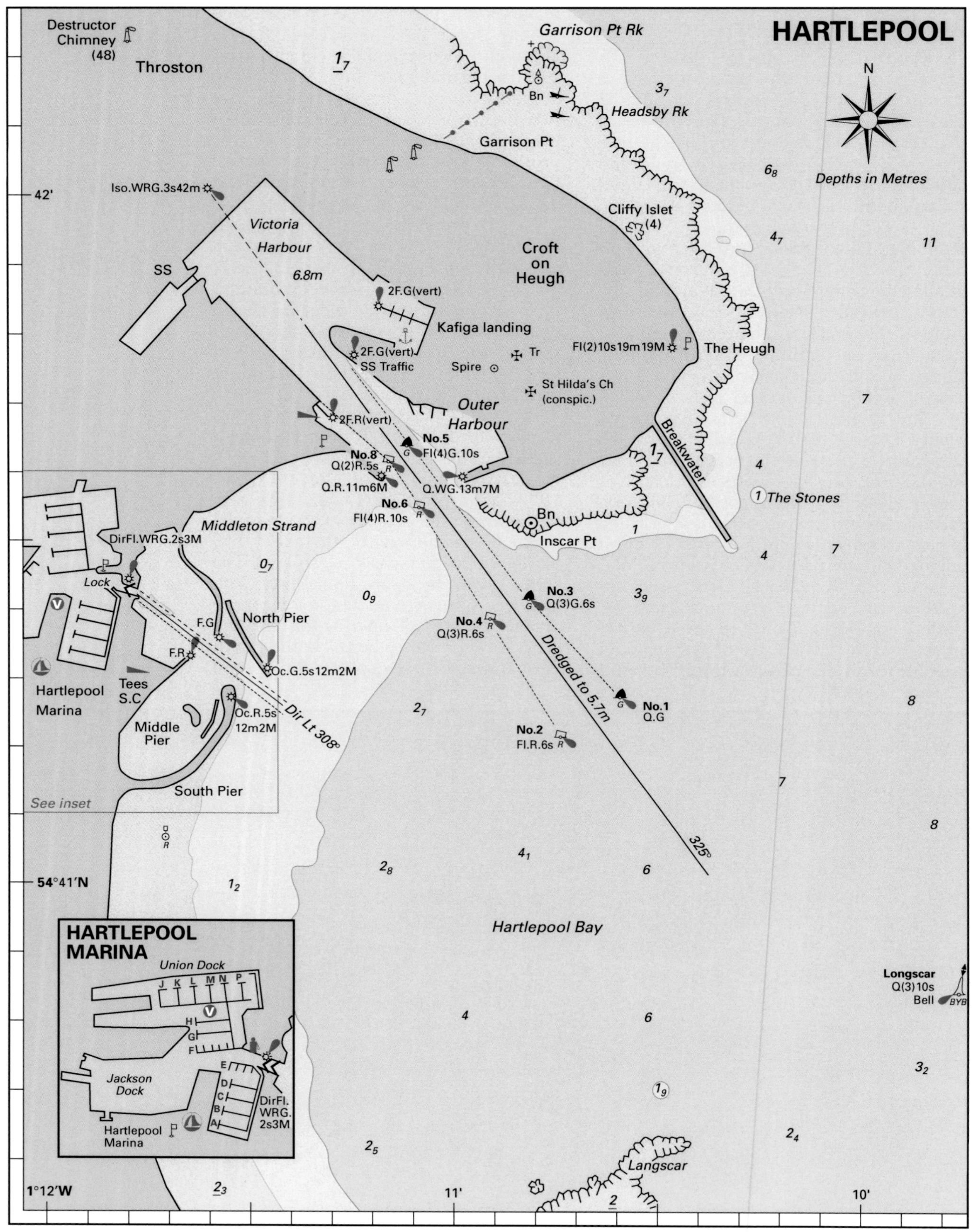
HARTLEPOOL
Depths in Metres
Destructor Chimney (48)
Throston
Garrison Pt Rk
Bn
Headsby Rk
Garrison Pt
Iso.WRG.3s42m
42'
Victoria Harbour
6.8m
SS
Cliffy Islet (4)
Croft on Heugh
2F.G(vert)
Kafiga landing
2F.G(vert)
SS Traffic
Tr
Spire
Fl(2)10s19m19M
The Heugh
St Hilda's Ch (conspic.)
Outer Harbour
2F.R(vert)
No.5
Fl(4)G.10s
No.8
Q(2)R.5s
Q.R.11m6M
Q.WG.13m7M
Breakwater
No.6
Fl(4)R.10s
The Stones
Bn
Inscar Pt
Middleton Strand
DirFl.WRG.2s3M
Lock
No.3
Q(3)G.6s
North Pier
F.G
No.4
Q(3)R.6s
F.R
Oc.G.5s12m2M
Dredged to 5.7m
Hartlepool Marina
Tees S.C
Dir Lt 308°
No.1
Q.G
Middle Pier
Oc.R.5s 12m2M
No.2
Fl.R.6s
South Pier
See inset
325°
54°41'N
Hartlepool Bay
HARTLEPOOL MARINA
Union Dock
Jackson Dock
DirFl. WRG. 2s3M
Hartlepool Marina
Longscar
Q(3)10s
Bell
Langscar
1°12'W
11'
10'

paper products. The Fish Quay, tucked away behind the Headland has naturally suffered with the decline of the industry in general, but it is still a flourishing concern. The western dock estate has been transformed into one of the largest marinas on the North Sea coast and it is surrounded by museum features, factory shop outlets, executive housing and a host of entertainment facilities that would not have seemed possible a decade ago. The Teesside Development Corporation was responsible for the transformation but it is now dissolved, its job done. The new management company, Hartlepool Renaissance, can in no way be accused of hyperbole in the selection of its title.

Approaches and entry

The Headland, by both day and night, makes identification very straightforward, though it must be noted that the Heugh lighthouse gives out a curiously weak light that is sometimes difficult to distinguish from surrounding shore lights.

From the south the only offlying danger is the Langscar which is marked at its outermost end by the Langscar E cardinal buoy. From the north the Heugh must be given a clearance of at least 2 cables to avoid the large skirt of rocks which surrounds the Headland. Strong winds from the east and southeast cause considerable broken water in the approaches.

Entry to the Victoria Basin is straightforward. The channel is marked by a series of lateral buoys and at night by a sector light (Iso.WRG.3s) on a leading line of 325°. The harbourmaster (✆ 01429 266127, VHF Ch 11) will advise as to whether there are any commercial shipping movements.

Entry to the Marina can also be made 24 hours a day provided that draught considerations permit (the lock can be called on ✆ 01429 865744 VHF Ch 37, 80 for advice). The entrance channel and lock cill have 0·8m at LAT, so shoal draught vessels will never be impaired. Most cruising yachts can regard 5 hours each side of HW as the feasible limits. The marina entrance bears 272° from No. 2 channel buoy and 294° from the Langscar buoy. There are sector lights (WRG.2s) for night approaches, the white sector being at 308°. Traffic lights are in operation; two red lights indicate that the lock is closed, one that a vessel is leaving. If forced to wait for a green light there is a pontoon outside the lock. Once inside the lock there is a pontoon to port so as to obviate the necessity for lock wall line control.

Moorings

In the centre of the Fish Quay section of the Victoria Basin is Kafiga Landing, a long pontoon which is jointly operated by the Tees and Hartlepool Yacht Club and the local Boat Owners Association. Vacant berths are usually available and arrangements can be made on arrival. The advantages of a mooring here are the low cost and the fact that it is in tidal water. Also, it is situated right in the heart of Old Hartlepool, a place of great charm and historic interest with several lively and traditional pubs. The disadvantage is that it is a considerable remove from town and there are very few facilities.

The cruising yachtsman who requires facilities will find them in abundance in the marina which has 500 berths and welcomes visiting craft. In 2015 the visitor rates were £1.95 per metre per day and £9.95 per metre per week, inclusive of VAT and electricity.

Facilties

Pre-renaissance Hartlepool was devoid of any facilities save sufficient water to float at all states of the tide. Even the harbour walls were dodgy. The town was about two miles from the moorings. The same is still more or less true of Kafiga Landing save the advantages of the pontoon berth. The new Hartlepool simply drips with facilities and most of them are remarkably convenient to access from the marina. In addition to the fuel, gas, electricity, water, trolleys and security associated with modern marinas Hartlepool has superb toilet and shower blocks on each side of the lockpit, both of which contain washing and drying machines. In addition there is a 300 ton travelhoist, the largest in Northern Europe, which operates 7 days a week, and other facilities for smaller lifts. There is a boatyard with all facilities for repair.

Near at hand on the Dock Estate are pubs, restaurants, hotel accommodation, the Tees and Hartlepool Yacht Club, shops (Asda), a seven screen cinema and a factory shopping mall at Jackson's Landing. For the visitor interested in maritime history there is the HMS *Trincomalee*, a restored frigate built in 1817 (the oldest boat afloat in Britain), a Maritime Museum and an Historic Quay – a reconstruction of an 18th century seaport which tells the story of dockside life and industry at the time of Cook and Nelson. A short distance beyond lies the railway station and that section of the town centre devoted to restaurants of many an ethnic hue. There is indeed a lot to do in Millennium Hartlepool. It merits inspection.

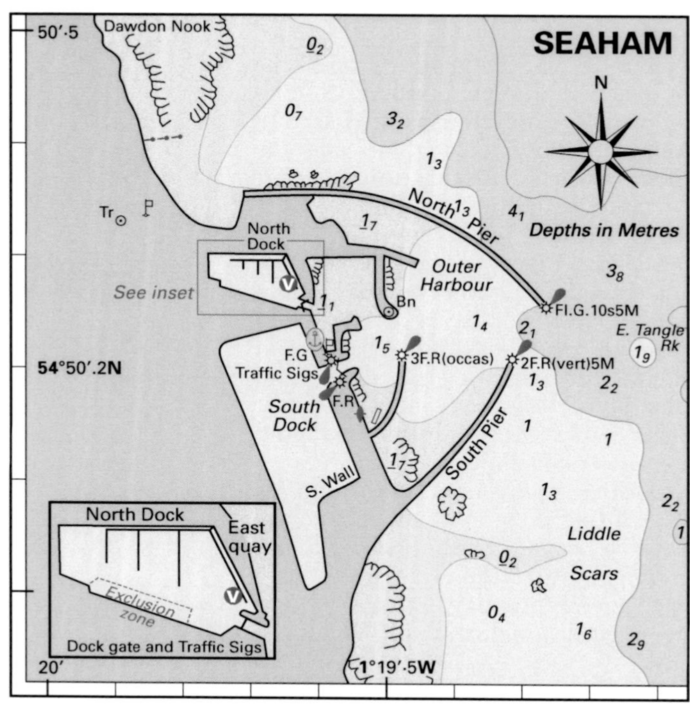

Seaham

Seaham Harbour stands as one of the finest monuments to the breathtaking insouciance that our early 19th century engineers exhibited towards challenges presented by nature. The Marquess of Londonderry, furious at being overcharged by the port of Sunderland for the export of coal from his Rainton pits, decided to build his own harbour. He simply picked the spot on the coast nearest to his collieries and threw together in three years, in the early 1830s, the mighty harbour that we can see and use to this day at Seaham. There was no estuary, not even a stream outlet worthy of note; there were no headlands or even rocky outcrops to afford protection; behind, there was simply a cliff face. Undeterred, Lord Londonderry's engineers did their own thing.

Seaham's continuing prosperity was able to outlive the inevitable decline of the Rainton pits because later mining technology enabled the concealed coalfield of East Durham to be exploited. Under the formidable capping of magnesian limestone the coal seams were thicker and more productive and two huge collieries were

Seaham harbour before the development of the North Dock marina *Airfotos*

Seaham marina

established at Seaham itself – Vane Tempest to the N and Dawdon to the S. Coal drops were constructed in the dock and until only a few years ago Seaham exhibited in microcosm the major themes of the economic history of County Durham. Now, sadly, the coal is no more and the harbour continues to operate as a general cargo port in a rather precarious way. There is still sufficient left, however, to mesmerize the historically inclined visitor and a night spent in Seaham is an unusual experience in this increasingly sanitised and homogenised world.

Approaches

The demise of the two great collieries to the north and south of the harbour has rendered Seaham perhaps less instantly recognizeable than it was a decade ago but the harbour itself is sufficiently prominent to present no problems with identification. The northern breakwater is surmounted by a conspicuous black and white striped lighthouse. A few rocky patches of 1–2m below LAT are indicated in the sketch chart in the immediate approaches but it is unlikely that a visitor would choose to make an entry into Seaham at such a time so the offing can be essentially regarded as clean.

View from Seaham harbour entrance

Seaham gate

Entry

Entry can be made with a vessel drawing 1·5m at any state of the tide but over the low water period there is no satisfactory alongside mooring that can be obtained. Both the outer and middle harbours shoal and dry away from the central dredged channel, so the only feasible solution if escape from the sea is of prime concern would be to anchor in the deeper parts.

The South Dock has tide gates. A level is made 2 hours before HW and the entrance remains open until 1 hour after HW. The harbourmaster's office (✆ 0191 5813246, VHF Ch 12) is manned from half an hour before this opening period until half an hour after, in addition to normal daytime office hours.

The North Dock, originally an enclosed dock used for coal export and more latterly a drying fish boat harbour, has in the past decade been developed into a marina which is open to vessels drawing up to 1·8m for three hours either side of HW. The marina entrance bears 276° from the outer harbour entrance, from which it is almost 350m. A single leaf hydraulic gate operates automatically around half tide to retain a depth of 1m to 1·8m over the low water period. Three red lights indicate that the gate is closed, three greens that it is safe to enter.

Ship entering Seaham

Moorings

The marina presently has a total of 70-odd pontoon berths, a minimum of three always kept available for visitors. These are the first berths encountered to the right of the entry gate, but the harbourmaster will allocate. The marina office (✆ 0191 5818998) is open during normal office hours. Outside these times, when the gate is open, contact can be made on 0785 5578836 or by calling VHF Ch 80, callsign *Seaham Marina*.

Pontoon services include electricity and water located along the walkways, access to which is gained via an electronic fob security system. Visitor rates in 2015 were £12.00 per day up to 7m, £15.00 per day for 7–10m, fees which include VAT and the use of electricity and water.

Facilities

The Marina Office is adjacent to the access ramp, situated on the first floor of the Waterside building which also contains toilets, showers, cafés and several other small business outlets. For more substantial stores it is but a short walk up the hill to the marina entrance which is a mere 100m. from Byron Place shopping centre, which includes a large Asda store, and from Church Street, the main shopping street of this compact little town. There is a railway station 1km to the W, with hourly services to Hartlepool, Teeside, Sunderland and Newcastle.

Sunderland

One could be forgiven for thinking that the fortress harbours of County Durham had been in place since the Crusades. They blend in with natural rock ramparts in the fashion of the great castles of the Welsh Marches. Yet they were not even there at the time of the Napoleonic threat. As late as the 1840s the only real improvements on the natural silted meandering outlet of the Wear were two rather vulnerable 18th century piers more or less in the positions occupied by the Inner Piers today. They were exposed to damage from the sea and from shipping, and the growing demands from coal owners and exporters, and the rapidly developing shipbuilding industry resulted in a massive port development in the mid-19th century. Indeed, it was competition from elsewhere that stimulated the urgency. The old enemy, Tyne, was in a similar state of torpor, but Lord Londonderry's harbour at nearby Seaham opened in 1831 and burgeoning coal export facilities at Hartlepool and Middlesbrough provided an even greater threat. Sir Hedworth Williamson of Whitburn, a north bank coal owner, had constructed the Wearmouth Dock (the remains of which are now the North Dock) in 1839 but it was on such a small scale that it was known as 'Sir Hedworth's bath tub'. It was financial backing in the bulky shape of the 'Railway King', George Hudson, that tipped the balance. In 1845 he was elected

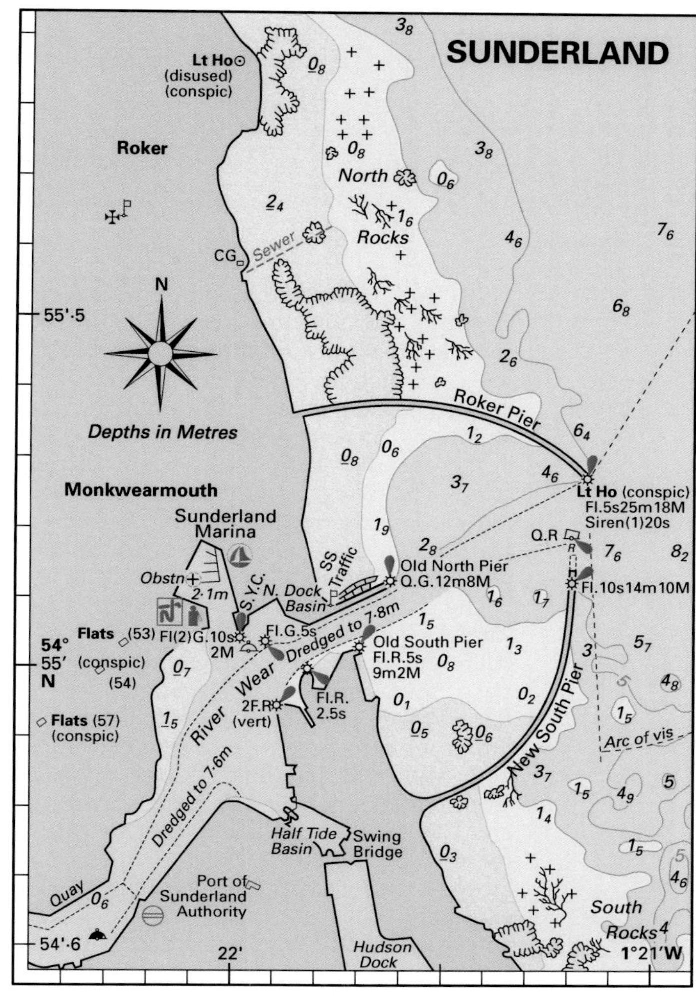

Sunderland
Airfotos

Sunderland approaches

as MP for Sunderland, and he embarked on vigorous promotion of his already considerable railway interests by backing the construction, on the foreshore, of the South Docks – a truly amazing and ambitious exercise which resulted, in 1850, in the opening of the docks as we see them today. The two great protective breakwaters followed in the second half of the century, and dredging completed the creation of a port 'wondrous to behold'.

The decline of coal export and shipbuilding during the 20th century is, of course, a recurrent theme along this coast, but Sunderland has demonstrated a remarkable ability to react, converting itself into a modern port with facilities for liquid and dry bulk handling, forest products, steel, containers, general cargo, ship repair and engineering. These activities are catered for in specialised sections of the South Docks and Corporation Quay, thus excluding pleasure craft activities. The entrance basin of 'Sir Hedworth's bath tub', however, remains as the North Dock with a modern and attractive yachting facility.

Approaches and entry

The sheer size of Sunderland, with tower blocks and port furniture, makes identification simple and the magnitude of the breakwaters, the N or Roker one surmounted with a vast red and white lighthouse, gives a seal of certainty to the approach. The only hazard in the offing is the Hendon Rock which has only a metre of water on top of it at LAT. It is situated 6 cables off the old disused S entrance so the navigator needs to be diligent if approaching at low water. The North Pier light has an arc to aid night approach – if it is visible when approaching from the north, the vessel is clear of Whitburn Steel. The arc is not so useful in clearing dangers when approaching from the south.

Entry between the breakwaters is simple at all states of the tide, though an underwater section of the southern breakwater (New South Pier) is indicated by a red can buoy which must be left to port. Entry signals are on the old North Pier at the entrance to the harbour proper. Three flashing red lights (vert) prohibit entry or departure. No lights means entry is permitted. The harbourmaster (✆ 0191 5140411, VHF Ch 14) will advise if in doubt. Alternatively, head for the marina in N dock (✆ 0191 5144721, VHF Ch 37, callsign *Sunderland Marina*) which is manned 24/7 throughout the year.

Moorings

The North Dock (the 'bath tub') has long provided excellent mooring facilities for pleasure craft in the port of Sunderland. Two clubs – the Sunderland Yacht Club and the Wear Boating Association – shared it for many years and the welcome was always warm. Now, however, a new marina has been established there with over 80 fully serviced pontoon berths and many more fore-and-aft moorings all in a minimum depth of 2·2m Charges for visitors in 2015 were on a sliding scale ranging from £15.00 per day for a 6m vessel to £24.00 per day for a 10m vessel.

Facilities

The marina has all modern facilities – power, water, fuel, toilets, showers, trolleys and wheeliebins, and based in the Marine Activities Centre are an Italian restaurant, a café and the WBA bar. Access is controlled and CCTV cameras are omnipresent. The visitor will, however, be tempted to peer out of this self-sufficient world when he realises that outside there are shops, pubs, an attractive beach just N of the breakwater and a regular bus service to the city centre one mile away for more sophisticated requirements. An unusual attraction nearby is the National Glass Centre, a short walk upriver through the university's St Peter's campus. This shows the history of glassmaking in Britain, an activity in which Sunderland has been preeminent since the days of the Venerable Bede.

The Wear is navigable for about 6 miles upriver to Cox Green, where shallow draught boats can lie afloat, The river is now no longer dredged through the former shipbuilding yards, which are now being 'landscaped' in a way which makes for an insipid sort of prettiness but has nothing like the fascination of the days when the Wear yards launched ships for the world.

River Tyne

Situated at the eastern end of Hadrian's Wall and at the lowest bridging point of the Tyne, the site that was later to become Newcastle was of critical importance to the Romans in their constant northward probing. Large forts were established where Newcastle and South Shields lie today and there is evidence of Roman port activity at both places. This activity flourished throughout the Saxon and Mediaeval periods culminating in the establishment, in 1492, of the Newcastle Trinity House to regulate pilotage and improve navigation on the river and approaches. This predated the London Trinity House by several decades. From this time coal began to loom large in the export trade of the Tyne. Local pits and adits were mined and the coals were transported to crudely built staithes on the river bank whence they were transferred to rowing keels and so to the larger collier brigs at anchor in deeper water. The coal trade from Tyne to London long predated the Industrial Revolution and was a key feature in the history of English shipping and shipbuilding.

It is rather surprising, given the development of docks and facilities in other ports from the late 18th century, that the Tyne failed to respond to the increasing demands of traders and shipowners. Perhaps the natural advantages of the Tyne stifled the need for such innovation or perhaps the tight and conservative stranglehold exercised by the Newcastle Corporation prevented initiative from flourishing. Whatever the case, there were no significant improvements before 1850, despite detailed suggestions from the engineer John Rennie as early as 1816. The river still pursued its natural course, hampered by sandbanks, spilling its power over areas of mudflat, or 'slakes' and pouring, untutored, into the sea at Tynemouth Bar.

By 1850 it was clear that something had to be done. The demand for coal and steel was accelerating; ships were being built ever larger and powered by steam engines which required engineering operations on a scale hitherto unknown; port developments at Hull, Hartlepool, Seaham and even the loathed Sunderland were burgeoning. The leviathans of Newcastle eventually stirred from their lethargy and a vast programme of

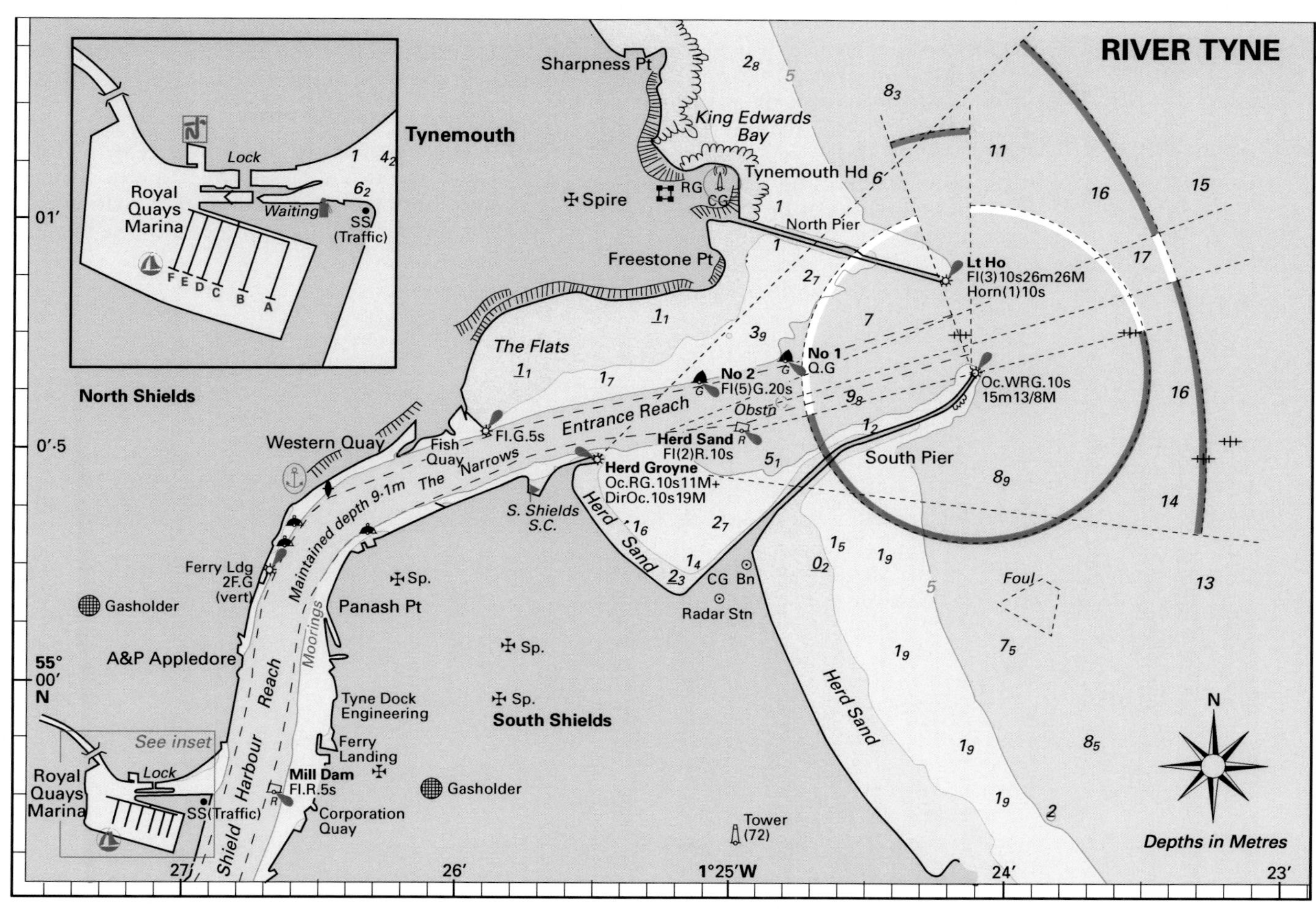

river improvement began. The entrance was protected by massive breakwaters, wet docks and graving docks were constructed, quays and coaling staithes were built and dredging was effected. In 1874 the low stone bridge at Newcastle was removed and replaced by a swing bridge, thus allowing seagoing vessels to proceed upriver. One immediate consequence was the construction of the Dunston coal staithes upstream, allowing for the efficient shipment of coals from the NW Durham field. Armstrong's Engine and Ordnance Works at Elswick were able to expand, confident that the largest of guns or machinery could be loaded onto ships at the back door. The Tyne finally achieved its potential, at the end of the 19th century, of being the maritime-industrial powerhouse of England.

This rather narrow and specialised industrial base, however, made the area vulnerable when depression and technological change hit again and again throughout the middle decades of the 20th century. With the exception of the wartime boom in production, Tyneside became a watchword for unemployment and urban-industrial decay. The coal trade declined to nothing; shipbuilding, in the face of global competition, shrank to a shadow of its former self; even heavy engineering, shorn of its local markets, followed suit. It is a tribute to the efforts of government, both national and local, that by the end of the 20th century the port of Tyne was able to turn itself around and develop commercial facilities in keeping with the new millennium.

The commercial port has been concentrated downstream, with the RoRo ferry facilities on the North Shields side being complemented to the south by the vast cargo handling concentrations at Tyne Dock and Riverside Quay. Here is situated a container terminal, a grain terminal, a bulk terminal and a huge car terminal where Jarrow Slake once lay. If the Venerable Bede were alive to look out of his vestry window today he would see gleaming lines of Nissan cars not a hundred yards away. An intelligent man, he would no doubt ruefully record that the Japanese had replaced the Vikings as the principal marauding force. He would be wrong, however, for these Nissans are all made in Sunderland and are heading for the world beyond the Tyne.

Farther upstream, the shipyards have greatly shrunk but Swan Hunters still hangs on at Wallsend and Cammel Lairds have a dry dock facility at Hebburn. Walker is home to the Offshore Technology Park, where rigs and supply vessels are built and serviced. Yet farther, the quays and industrial sites towards Newcastle have largely gone and the river has been landscaped as a public amenity. The Quayside in the centre of the city itself has been restored in a pleasing way and there are few locations in Britain where one can moor a small yacht and feel so central to a city and to its intriguing history.

Approaches and entry

The approaches to the Tyne are, seaward of the magnificent pier heads, totally clear of any obstruction whether the visitor is a yachtsman or the captain of a cruise liner. In

Tyne approaches

The mouth of the Tyne. Note the miles of quay space at Fish Quay

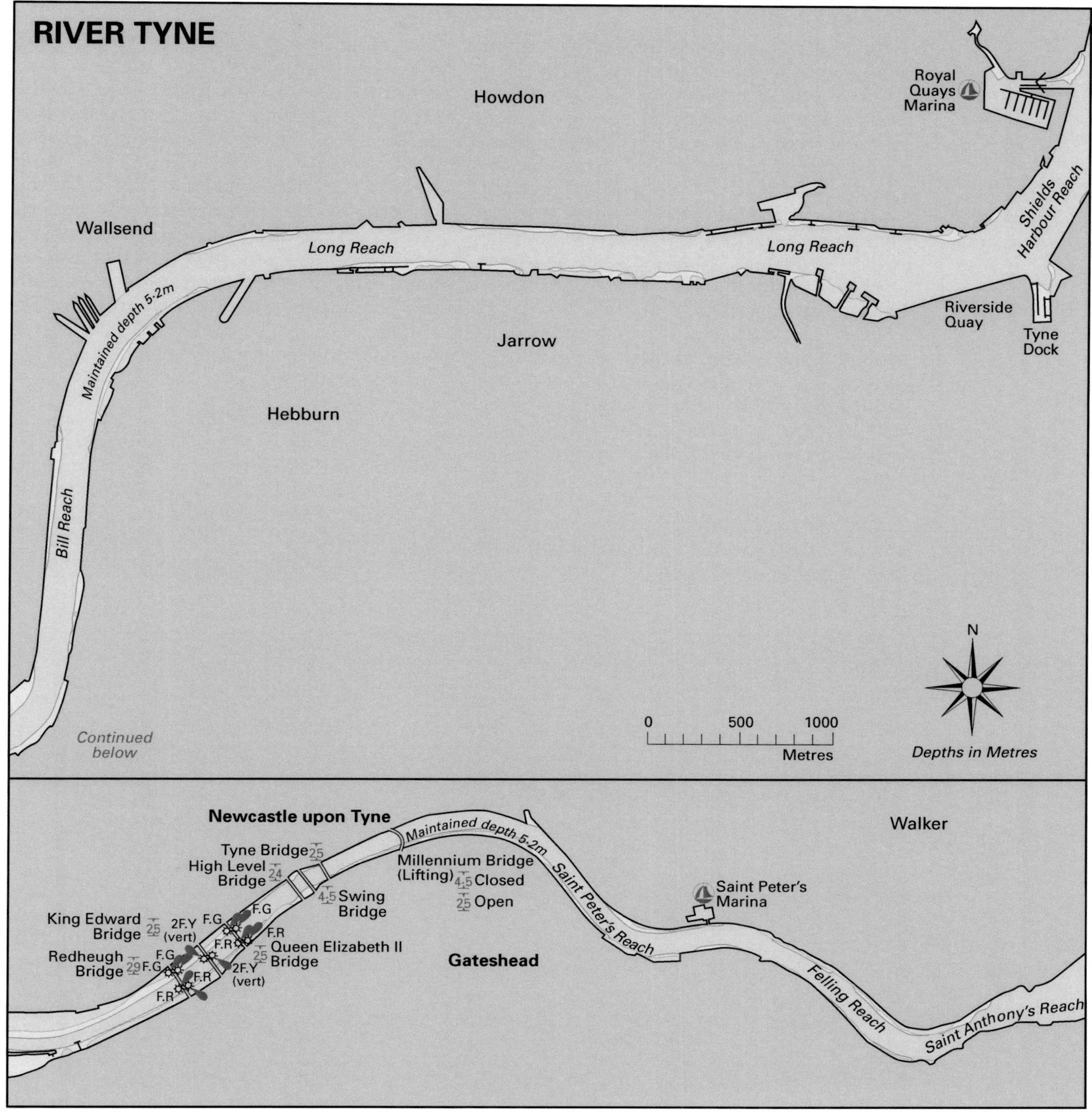

addition they are very conspicuous. To the north, the entrance is dominated by the high ground of Tynemouth, with its castle and priory remains and a beetling monument to Admiral Lord Collingwood; to the south, albeit a mile farther inland, the conspicuous Lawe of South Shields provides the rampart. The entrance itself is wide and deep and at night leading lights from the North Shields lighthouse (258°) can be seen for twenty miles offshore in good visibility. To give an even greater seal of certainty, at night the lights on both the Inner and Outer Shields piers are sectored. 'Twould be a foolish mariner indeed who made a hash of the Tyne'. It must be noted, however, that in severe weather from any easterly direction the seas at the entrance can break in a confused fashion, especially against an ebb tide. Information on shipping movements may be obtained from Tyne Harbour Radio (✆ 0191 257 0407, VHF Ch 12).

Moorings and facilities

There are many mooring possibilities for the visitor to the Tyne.

Entrance anchorages

A small craft may safely anchor on a good sandy bottom either behind the North Pier, from where an exploration of Tynemouth can be effected, or behind the South Pier, fronting Herd Sand, which will afford direct access to the town centre of South Shields. These anchorages can only be recommended in fairly settled weather but they provide very real strategic options for the passage maker who wants to sit out a tide and have a beer rather than penetrate time-consumingly upstream.

There are yacht clubs, mainly concerned with dinghy racing, at both these places. Tynemouth is a pleasant and elegant spot with a delightful selection of rocky caves and beaches to explore. South Shields is a very substantial town, which offers a total range of urban facilities and a variety of historic memorabilia. For the connoisseur of curry, the road from the anchorage to the town centre, Ocean Rd, is wall to wall with fine Bengali restaurants.

North Shields Fish Quay

This is an interesting, if sometimes robust mooring option. The quays were constructed on a fairly grand scale and the reduction of fishing activity in the last two decades has meant that there is always plenty of space available clear of the fishing boats. The tidal rise and fall and the industrial nature of the quay walls must be dealt with by careful fendering but it is a worthwhile endeavour for the run ashore is good. Chandlers and chart shops are useful, but perhaps the essence of the place is the variety of quayside taverns. The roisterer will no doubt feel happier here than in a safe and sanitised marina.

The Royal Quays Marina

Slightly less than a mile upstream of the North Shields river ferry pontoon, and exactly opposite to the South Shields one, is the former Albert Edward dock, now totally redeveloped into the Royal Quays Marina. The sector lock gates operate at all states of

Royal Quays, North Shields Fish Quay and mouth of the Tyne *Airfotos*

the tide and are manned 24 hours a day. There are fully serviced pontoon berths for 200 craft and there is plenty of space to expand as demand increases. Visitors can inform the marina of an intended arrival (✆ 0191 272 8282, VHF Ch 80) or, if no contact is immediately possible, simply tie up on the waiting pontoon outside the lock and await instruction. Craft too large for pontoon berths can easily be accommodated safely and securely on the quay walls inside the dock. Fuel, chandlery, travelhoist, shower and laundry facilities are handily available. *The Earl of Zetland* serves as a floating pub/restaurant.

An advantage of a Royal Quays mooring is the total security that is afforded in an area where, sadly, it has been traditionally necessary. The visitor will be able to leave his boat here as long as he requires and is able to afford, confident that it will come to no harm. Visitors fees in 2015 were £2.55 per metre per day (minimum charge £20.00) with a 50% discount after 5 days (VAT included).

A disadvantage, for some, will be the isolation from non-marina activities. To the south, upstream, is the International Ferry Terminal, which, although providing excellent road access, acts as a complete social and scenic brick wall. To the west and north the former industrial areas have been completely 'landscaped' and developed with two rather swish housing areas separated by a linear park. It provides a pleasant and relaxing environment for the resident boat owner but is a trifle 'thin' for the mariner with a yen to strut his stuff.

St Peters Marina

(✆ 0191 265 4472, VHF Ch 80, 37)

Seven and a half miles inland from the Tyne entrance, St Peters is clearly disadvantaged compared with Royal Quays in attracting the passing visitor or indeed as a permanent base for yachtsmen keen on offshore

Approaching the Royal Quays lock pit

St Peter's Marina

activity. It has, however, an overwhelming advantage with regard to being a secure base from which to explore the splendours of the city of Newcastle. When to this is added the demand from non-sailing craft and its proximity to navigation on the Tyne above Newcastle, then a marina at St Peters makes very good sense indeed.

Hewn out of the land during the redevelopment of redundant commercial quay space, the marina accommodates 150 boats and can handle visiting craft up to 80ft in length and drawing up to 10ft. There are no lock gates but the dock depth is maintained by a cill 0·8m below Chart Datum. This means in effect that at spring tides, a vessel drawing 1·5m will have to wait for a maximum of 2 hours at the

The former Albert Edward dock, now the Royal Quays Marina

outside waiting berth. At neap tides there will be low water access.

There are full marina facilities and the marina is manned 24/7 all year round. Electricity and water are laid on to pontoons and petrol and diesel are available at the fuelling berth. Laundry, showers, toilets, brokerage and chandlery complete the full modern marina picture. Mooring fees for visitors in 2015 were £0.60 per foot per day (excl. VAT). A pub/restaurant, the Fog on the Tyne, provides a useful on-the-spot service, and shops will feature in further developments, but the visitor in search of interest and action will not be deprived in the interim for Newcastle city centre is only a mile upstream. A half-hourly bus service is available to plug this gap in inclement weather.

The Quayside

The visitor can now safely moor in the historic heart of Newcastle much more safely and conveniently than in past years. A new security controlled visitors pontoon has been installed outside the Pitcher and Piano pub immediately downstream of the new Millennium Bridge. This is a city council facility and the procedure is slightly unusual. The visiting yachtsman must tie up to the pontoon, walk up the gangway, press a button and speak to an office-based operative who will emerge to assist. Bars and restaurants abound in the Quayside area, though it would be a visitor with specialised taste who would put himself there on a Friday or Saturday night when the Bigg Market Brigade is on the rampage. At quieter times, however, it is a quite spectacular and fascinating place to moor, with the bridges, castle, cathedral, Central Station, museums and all the stately 19th century urban architecture of Grainger, Dobson and Clayton arrayed as far as the eye can see and the foot can travel. It is fortunate indeed that T. Dan Smith in the mid 20th century did not have time to effect improvements on the work of his predecessors. This scene could not be improved.

Upriver

The Swing Bridge and the new Millennium pedestrian bridge have headroom for 4·6m at MHWS. They both swing, giving masted access at 24 hours notice, but it is hard to imagine a visitor going to this trouble to savour four miles of industrial and urban riverfront before being confronted by Scotswood Bridge with 7·6m. For the mastless mariner, however, there are attractive upriver destinations. He can cruise on past Blaydon and Ryton as far as Wylam depending on draught and tide. A pilgrimage to Stephenson's cottage at Wylam makes a fitting end to a dramatic journey through two centuries of industrial and transport history.

Newcastle, floating pontoons below Millennium Bridge

Seaton Sluice

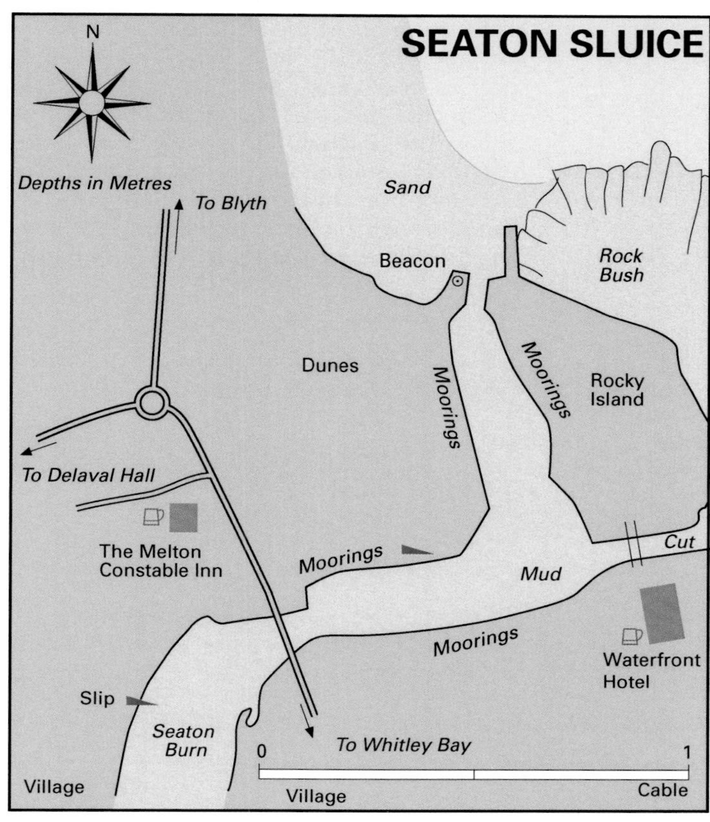

There is something secretive and surprising about this little port, tucked around a rocky corner about a mile N of St Mary's Island. As a coal exporting port it flourished until the second half of the 19th century, when it was eclipsed in this function by the development of Blyth, some three miles across the bay to the north. This eclipse has been repeated in the spheres of fishing and pleasure boating, and few cruising yachtsman would forsake the welcome and facilities offered by Blyth and turn aside to investigate Seaton Sluice. Yet it is a fascinating place and, given the right weather, makes for a rewarding stop.

The Delaval family arrived with William the Conqueror and established their baronial seat nearby. In the early 18th century they discovered substantial deposits of coal under their estate so they commissioned Vanbrugh, architect of Blenheim Palace and Castle Howard, to build them an impressive family seat at Delaval Hall so that they could more closely supervise the creation of their wealth. They constructed a weir across the Seaton Burn, near the mouth, which they closed to pond

Seaton Sluice
Airfotos

back the waters of the burn to be released at low water to scour the harbour of sand and silt. A pier and harbour walls were constructed and coal export flourished for 200 years. Indeed, 22 sailing ships are recorded at one time as having Seaton Sluice as a home port. In the 1760s a deep cut was made through the rock to the east to avoid the difficult north-facing entrance but this did not prove to be a great success. The growing size of ships and the development of better facilities at Blyth and on the Tyne spelled the end of this trade in the later 19th century.

Diligent though the Delaval family were at exploiting their fortune, the later members became notorious for playboy gaiety. The jokes they perpetrated on their unfortunate house guests included beds that suddenly dropped through the floor into tanks of water, and sliding walls between guests' chambers which could suddenly be withdrawn to leave the guests in full view in their nether garments or in flagrento. The last male of this intriguing family died in the 19th century by being kicked in the privates by a laundrymaid he was attempting to molest. Such stories serve to lure the more curious yachtsman towards the quays of Seaton Sluice.

Approaching Seaton Sluice

Seaton Sluice from entrance looking in

Seaton Sluice entrance in an easterly

Approaches

From the south, Rocky Island – formed by the Delavals' attempt to create a second harbour entrance – must be given a reasonable berth as there is a skirt of rocks on its northern and eastern sides. Indeed the only approach is the one along the beach from the north. From this direction the new eastern breakwater is visible.

Entry and moorings

There is about 3m at the entrance at MWHS. This means, in effect, that a vessel drawing 1·5m is restricted to a HW entry at neaps but can allow 1 hour either side at springs. The deepest water in the entrance can be found by lining up the first section of the eastern quay and sticking close to it until the harbour widens. Depths slowly shoal inside the harbour and towards the wall moorings.

Deeper draught vessels are advised to moor in the first (N–S) section of the harbour, against a wall as space is available. The local authority have provided a surfeit of good wall ladders. Shoaler craft can proceed farther up harbour into the E–W section where there are once again moorings on either hand.

Facilities and diversions

Tyneside suburban sprawl has started to envelop the place but the area around the harbour retains a certain charm with shops, three pubs, and fish and chips at hand. To invoke the curious history of this little port it is necessary to stroll a mile inland to the magnificent hall. It is only occasionally open to the public but thoughts of beds in baths, sliding walls and chambermaids will invariably bring a smile to the lips.

Blyth

Home to the Royal Northumberland Yacht Club for over 100 years, Blyth has long been synonymous with Tyneside pleasure boating. This is slightly surprising, for during that time the port has had a very busy commercial history and it is a sad fact that until very recently, when marinas have become big business, commercial port operators were inclined to view pleasure craft with something less than enthusiasm. This has never been so at Blyth where the commerce, the fishing and the pleasure boating have coexisted happily over an extensive period of time.

The mouth of the River Blyth had long been used for the shipping of local coal before the industry's decline but prior to the mid-19th century it was simply an undeveloped river mouth operable only in the top half of the tide. The construction of quays and piers and the dredging of the newly-channelled river mouth led to incredibly rapid development, and the rise to prominence of the nearby ironworks at Bedlington served to accelerate the demand for facilities. By the early part of the 20th century Blyth was the busiest coal port in Europe, a position retained until the 1960s.

Nowadays the ironworks and coal mines are long gone and all that remains are some open cast workings further to the north, which provide residual shipments of coal to the Thames. The massive high level coaling staith at Cambois in the north of the harbour was demolished during the 1990s, as was the Cambois power station whose chimneys have long been a homing signal for the sailors of Blyth. The principal trade is now the export of scrap and grain and the import of fertilizer, chemicals, logs, plywood and paper, all this activity taking place at upriver wharves. The western quay in South Harbour houses a container terminal which has a RoRo facility adjacent. Immediately to the south of this is the Fish Quay which is home to a couple of dozen local trawlers and seasonally plays host to a number of Scottish visitors. Adjacent, in the eastern section of the South Harbour is the home of the RNYC thus completing the ongoing picture of peaceful maritime coexistence.

Approaches and entry

From the south, the approaches are clear and the Fairway Buoy will be easily identified. From here, leading lights (324°) lead directly through the piers and up the river but the fairway is wide and clean with beacons on either hand.

From the north, two long bushes of rock, the Sow and Pigs and Seaton Sea Rocks lie to seaward of the East Pier. These dry, but must be avoided at all times, even at HW. There used to be a useful Sow and Pigs buoy to indicate a clear line to the pier end but this is now gone. It is not necessary to go all the way to the Fairway Buoy but precise judgement on cutting the corner must be left to the individual. It is more precise at night for there is a fixed red sector on the lower light of the lighthouse at the end of the E pier. An approaching vessel must leave the red sector before proceeding towards the harbour entrance.

A submerged training wall on the W side of the harbour entrance is a hazard to note. Its end is marked by a dolphin topped with a red light.

Yachts in Blyth South harbour at the RNYC moorings *David Ford*

Blyth Harbour entrance from North Blyth *David Ford*

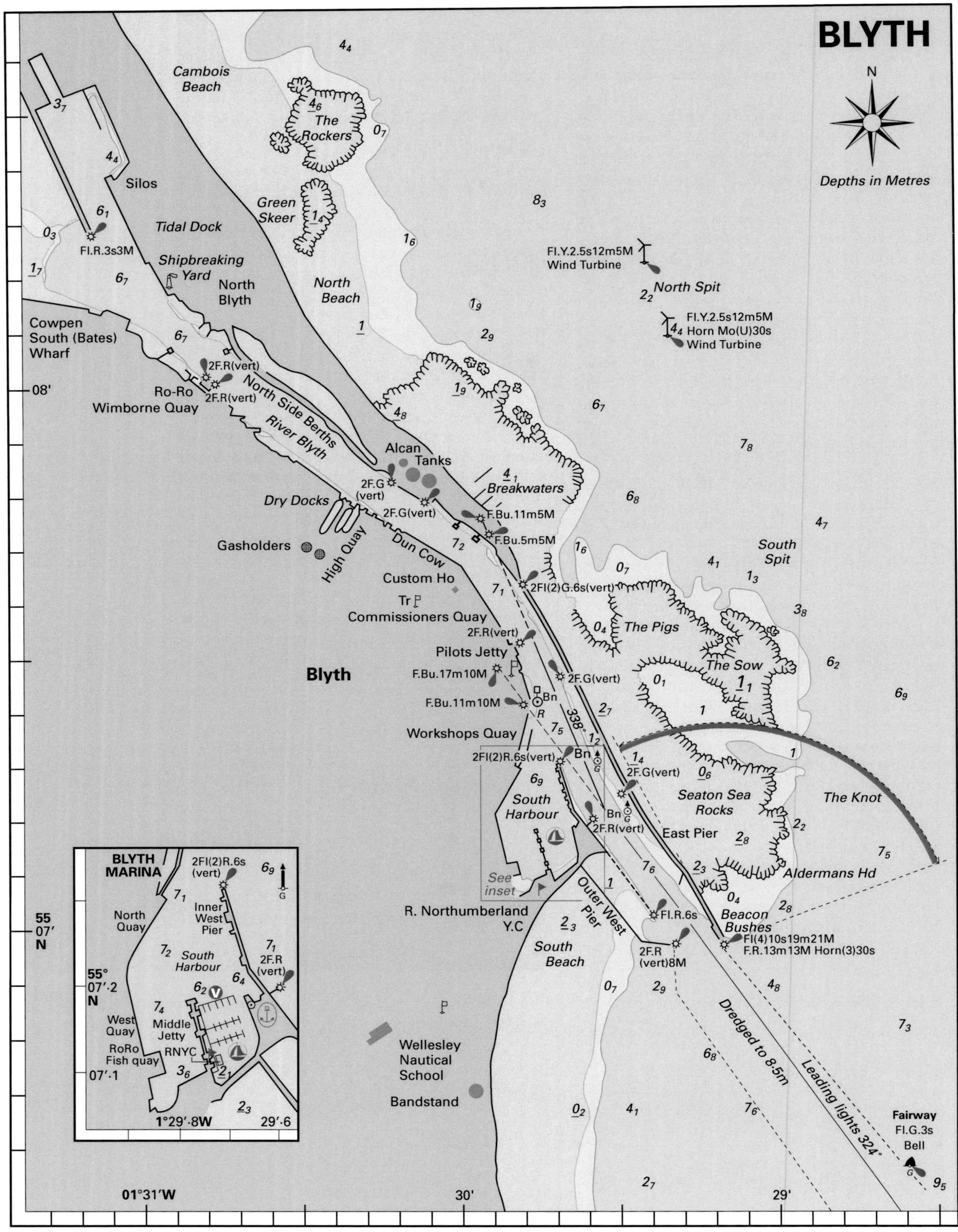
BLYTH
N
Depths in Metres
Cambois Beach
The Rockers
Green Skeer
Silos
Tidal Dock
Fl.R.3s3M
Shipbreaking Yard
North Blyth
North Beach
Cowpen South (Bates) Wharf
Ro-Ro Wimborne Quay
2F.R(vert)
North Side Berths
River Blyth
Alcan Tanks
Breakwaters
2F.G (vert)
2F.G(vert)
F.Bu.11m5M
F.Bu.5m5M
Dry Docks
Gasholders
High Quay
Dun Cow
Custom Ho
Tr
Commissioners Quay
2F.R(vert)
Pilots Jetty
Blyth
F.Bu.17m10M
F.Bu.11m10M
Bn
Workshops Quay
2Fl(2)R.6s(vert)
2Fl(2)G.6s(vert)
2F.G(vert)
338°
Fl.Y.2.5s12m5M Wind Turbine
North Spit
Fl.Y.2.5s12m5M Horn Mo(U)30s Wind Turbine
South Spit
The Pigs
The Sow
Seaton Sea Rocks
The Knot
East Pier
Aldermans Hd
South Harbour
See inset
R. Northumberland Y.C
Outer West Pier
Fl.R.6s
2F.R (vert)8M
Beacon Bushes
Fl(4)10s19m21M F.R.13m13M Horn(3)30s
South Beach
Dredged to 8·5m
Leading lights 324°
Wellesley Nautical School
Bandstand
Fairway Fl.G.3s Bell
08'
55 07' N
01°31'W
30'
29'
BLYTH MARINA
2Fl(2)R.6s (vert)
North Quay
Inner West Pier
South Harbour
2F.R (vert)
55° 07'·2 N
West Quay
Middle Jetty
RoRo Fish quay
RNYC
07'·1
1°29'·8W
29'·6

Moorings

Most visiting yachts will choose to moor in the South Harbour where the RNYC have their headquarters in the east basin. There is deep water all over the harbour so no draught problems will be encountered at any state of the tide. The club have recently laid pontoon moorings and visitors should moor initially to the northern side of the northern pontoon before inquiring further of club members. The HQ of the club is a former Calshot Spit LV moored at the southern end of this basin.

The harbour is navigable much farther than the South Harbour entrance. Deep water lasts for another couple of miles up to the former Cambois coal drops, and beyond this the River Blyth is navigable at HW as far as Bedlington for shallow draught vessels. There are no satisfactory moorings in the commercial section but in the drying section at the northern end of town the River Blyth Boating Association has drying moorings and welcomes visitors.

Facilities

The members of the RNYC are legendarily friendly to visitors and their LV HQ (house yacht *Tyne*) has showers and a bar. Nearby there is a chandlery in the SW corner of South Harbour, together with a slipway, fuelling berth and repair facilities.

Shopping is not too convenient but it is only a mile to the town centre which has pubs, banks and a whole gamut of shops. It is not a town of great architectural interest though an unusual feature is the presence in the street of an 18th century lighthouse which used to serve as a lead in the days before the harbour was improved. Above all, Blyth is friendly.

Amble

Pedants and purists refer to the little port at the mouth of the Coquet as Warkworth Harbour. It is as though they are over anxious to reach the unsullied beaches of the N. Northumberland coast and choose to ignore that Amble is firmly of the Northumberland coalfield, albeit at its northern extremity. Local collieries and open cast workings used the quays at Amble as an export facility and the settlement grew in the fashion of mining villages everywhere – terraced houses with only a smattering of shops and facilities. The routes formerly followed by the railway lines to the staith can still be traced as gaps in the housing. Now, however, there are no lines, nor is there any coal export and the coal drops have been removed. There is not a great deal to recommend it as a village per se, but its situation with Coquet Island just offshore and the splendours of Warkworth Castle a short distance inland make it an interesting and popular port of call.

Amble with Coquet Island *Airfotos*

Approaches

The approaches to Amble are all about Coquet Island. St Cuthbert occupied his lonely hermit cell here when a tyro monk but he was hauled into the land of the living in AD684 by Elfreda, the abbess of Whitby, who persuaded him to succeed Aidan as the Bishop of Lindisfarne. The rocky isle, surmounted by its lighthouse gives a conspicuous pointer to the whereabouts of the port of Amble.

Until a few years ago, this section of the Northumberland coast from Blyth to Boulmer was well equipped with buoyage, marking the rocky 'stiles' and 'bushes' that abound here. In their wisdom, or more probably in their penury, Trinity House have removed them all so that the yachtsman is now forced to fend for himself.

An approach from the south was always interesting and scenic but also very safe when the narrow Coquet Channel was

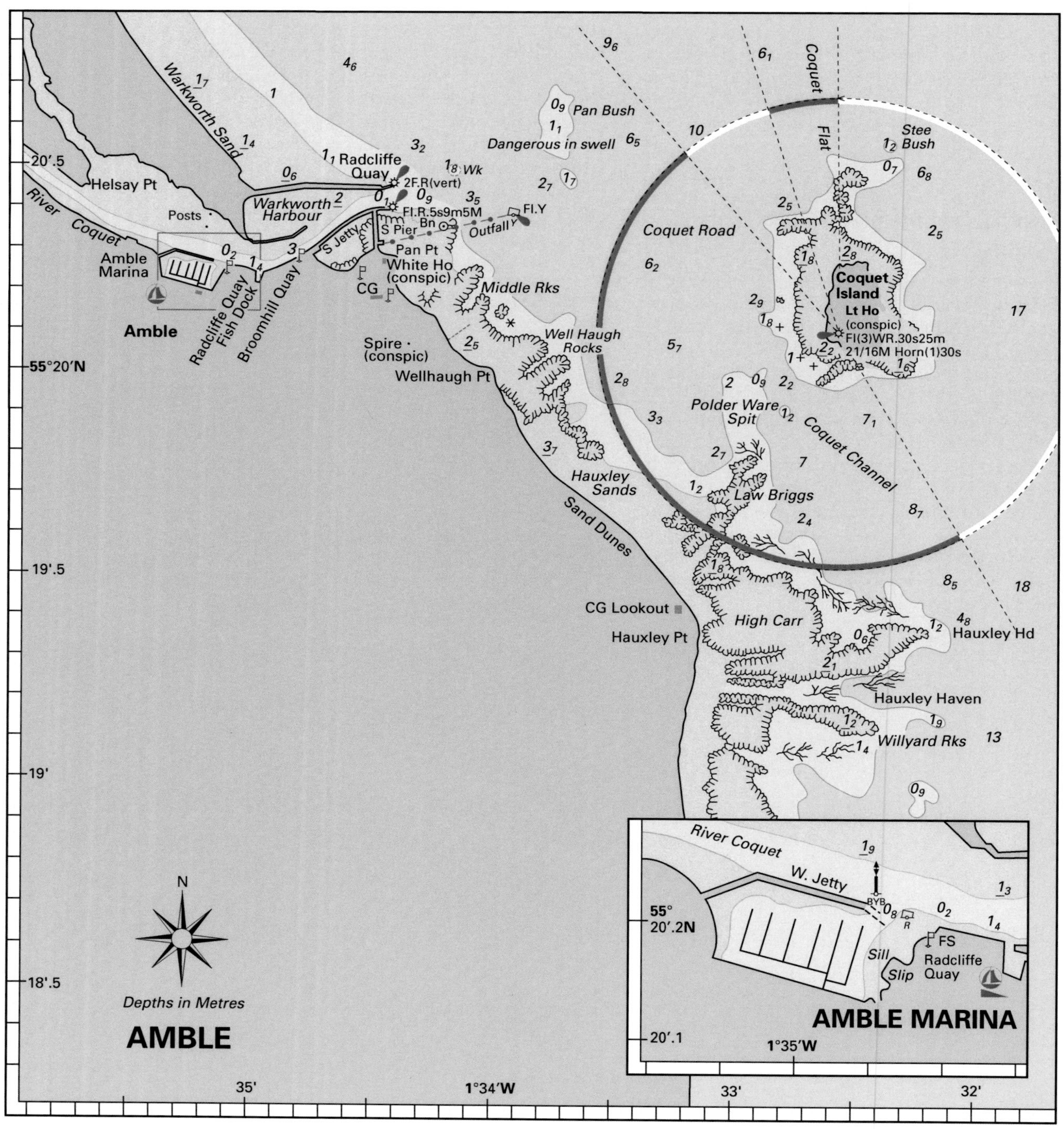

marked by the Hauxley and SW Coquet buoys. Now they are gone and more precise navigation is necessary. This I must leave to the yachtsman and his instruments but with the caution that it is dangerous at night or in poor visibility and that it is difficult in the lower half of the tide. In such adverse circumstances, or for those with a lack of experience and familiarity, it is advisable to pass outside of Coquet Island. Even here there are offlying rocks to be considered, both to the north of the island and at Pan Bush, irritatingly squatting right in the middle of Coquet Roads.

To pass between Coquet Island and Pan Bush, the white NW sector of the Coquet lighthouse is useful, whether coming from the north or from the south around Coquet Island. Mindful of the problems created by removing the buoyage, the authorities keep the light flashing all day. Once in the white sector, a vessel can be confident of avoiding Pan Bush, and if heading for the harbour an alignment of the red can sewer outfall buoy with the harbour entrance clears Pan Bush to the south.

From the north it is much more direct to pass between Pan Bush and the shore. Here an alignment of the two pier end lights gives the best approach.

Entry

The entrance to the Coquet is much subject to silting, and depths vary. The bar virtually dries at LWS, so a safe entry limit for a craft drawing 1·5m is 4 hours either side of HW. If there is a heavy swell caused by onshore winds, then it is wise to be more prudent with the limits. There is a lighthouse on each pier – the S one with RW stripes and the N on a white iron structure. If in any doubt about depths then advice can be obtained either from the harbourmaster (✆ 01665 710306, VHF Ch 14) or from Amble Marina (✆ 01665 712168, VHF Ch 80). Once inside, the best water lies along the S side, close to the quays.

Moorings

The Broomhill Quay, the first stretch of quay encountered, is frequently busy with fishing boats and even if it appears empty they may suddenly materialize in the middle of the night. The Radcliffe Quay, beyond the small drying Fish Dock, is much quieter. At all the quays, craft drawing 1·5m will take the bottom at LWS. The nature of the bottom varies so mastrope protection is recommended.

A more comfortable mooring can be had in Amble Marina, immediately W of Radcliffe Quay after leaving a red can buoy to port. The starboard side of the entrance is marked by an E cardinal beacon. There is a cill at the entrance which retains water in the marina and the depth on the cill is shown on a tide gauge at the entrance. This is 1m shallower than depths on the bar and in effect it means that a vessel drawing 1·5m can cross 3 hours 45 minutes either side of HWS and 4 hours either side of HWN.

Visitors should tie up at the end of the second pontoon, beside the fuel pumps, to receive berthing instructions. Visitor mooring fees for 2015 were £12.50 per metre per week and £2.50 per metre per day (includes VAT and Harbour Dues).

Coquet Island from the north

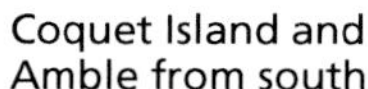

Coquet Island and Amble from south

Facilities

Normal marina facilities are available and there is at hand a substantial boatyard, slipway and chandlery, Harrisons Amble Boat Co. (✆ 01665 710267). There are shops and pubs in the village, though the focus of evening village life remains, in the best mining tradition, in the CIU club.

A pleasant walk of a mile upstream will lead to Warkworth castle, the first of the mighty Norman defensive castles of the Northumbrian coast as one journeys north. It towers over the village, situated in a great loop of the river which is crossed by a Norman bridge. Rowing boats are available for hire if the visitor is too weary to inflate his dinghy and do the whole trip by water. The village is extraordinarily pretty and is well equipped with pubs, shops and tea rooms. Warkworth is a must when berthed in Amble.

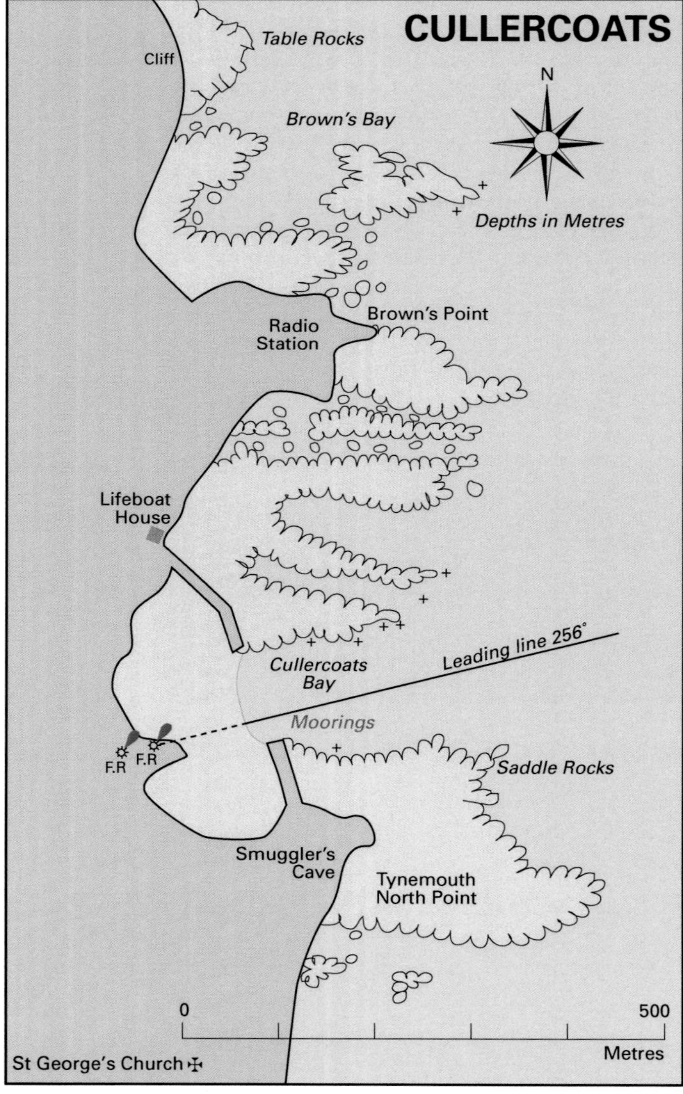

Northumberland coast anchorages

Cullercoats

Although buried in the commuter belt of the North Tyneside coast, this little harbour retains enough charm and seclusion to make an interesting sojourn and run ashore. In common with most spots in the North East where boat could make contact with sand, coal was exported in earlier times, but Cullercoats' reputation since the 18th century has revolved around fishing. As late as the early 20th century local cobles indulged in the seasonal herring fishery and the Cullercoats Fishwives roamed around Tyneside selling fish from 'creels' on their backs.

There is a small drying harbour which is essentially a beach naturally protected by headlands with rocky extensions and reinforced by small stone piers. The northern headland is conspicuous by the presence of Cullercoats radio station and the best water into the harbour is on a leading line (256°) formed by two conspicuous baskets (F red lights at night) on the cliff top. At HWS there is more than 5m at the entrance, decreasing up the beach. At LWS the harbour area dries out to the piers.

The sand inside is clean and soft and provides a safe anchorage over the HW period provided there is no onshore weather or swell. If a longer stay is planned, the visiting craft must be prepared to dry out, either on the beach if possessed of a suitable bottom or against the southern pier wall, taking care not to interfere with the activities of the few remaining cobles.

Ashore there are shops, pubs and cafés a-plenty, with an aquarium run by Newcastle University Marine Laboratory as an additional diversion. The harbour is close to a Metro station should crew change be necessary, and hard by the station is one of the most highly-recommended Bengali restaurants in the North East.

Newbiggin

Newbiggin is made conspicuous from the sea by its parish church perched on the headland of Newbiggin Point. This is one of only two 14th century spires in the whole of Northumberland though I am not certain that this esoteric circumstance will lure many visiting yachtsmen. More importantly, the headland gives shelter from the N through W to SW, encouraging local coble fishing and providing a pleasant anchorage when conditions are suitable.

Cullercoats lifeboat and Marine Laboratory

An approach must be made that clears the foul rocky ground off Newbiggin Point to the N and Spital Point to the S, but the beach area itself is clean and gentle of contour. An anchorage can be made in 2–3m off the end of the small breakwater at the N end of the beach.

Newbiggin used to be a locally popular seaside town, but the disappearance of a lot of the beach combined with cheap and accessible Mediterranean holidays has reduced its popularity in this respect. There remain, however, plenty of pubs and shops which will serve to revictual the passing yachtsman.

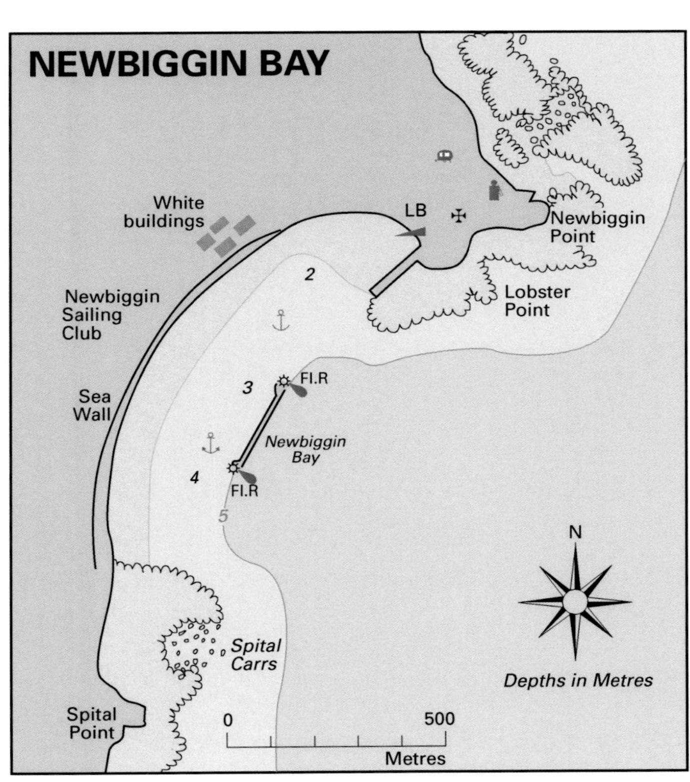

Newbiggin *Airfotos*

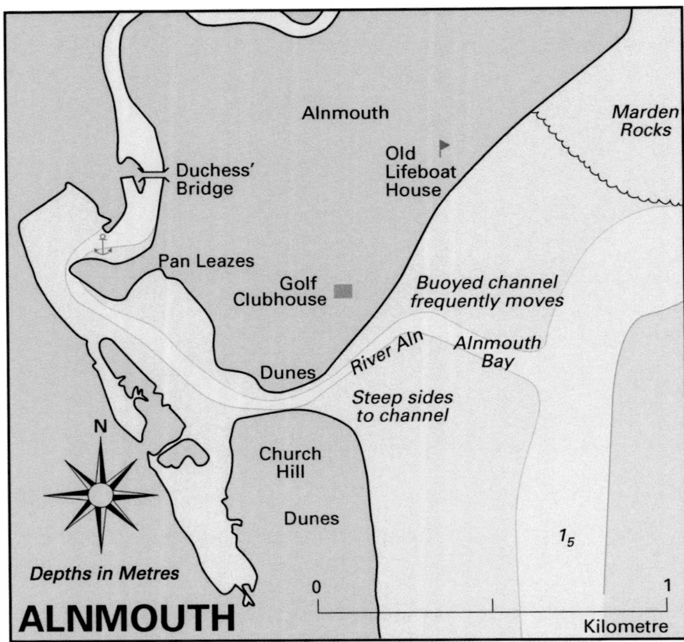

Alnmouth

From medieval times until the early 19th century, this harbour at the mouth of the Aln served in general as the port for Alnwick, but in particular for the export of local grain. Some of the fine 18th century granaries remain, now converted into hotels and apartments. In 1806 a storm altered the course of the river and the new outlet was prone to siltation, leading to the decline of trade throughout the 19th century. Today it retains a genteel holiday function with attractive golfing facilities and nearby Alnmouth station permits Tyneside commuting for the wealthy.

The estuary dries out at LW and there are no surviving quays. Alnmouth can, therefore, only be used over the HW period for a quick run ashore; otherwise vessels will take the ground albeit in conditions of perfect shelter. The village is conspicuous from sea and the river entrance lies between the village and Church Hill, a round topped dune to the S surmounted by a cross. The river channel across the beach is variable, according to prevailing sea conditions but the deepest water is usually indicated in summer by three port hand markers maintained by local boat owners.

Alnmouth *Airfotos*

Alnmouth

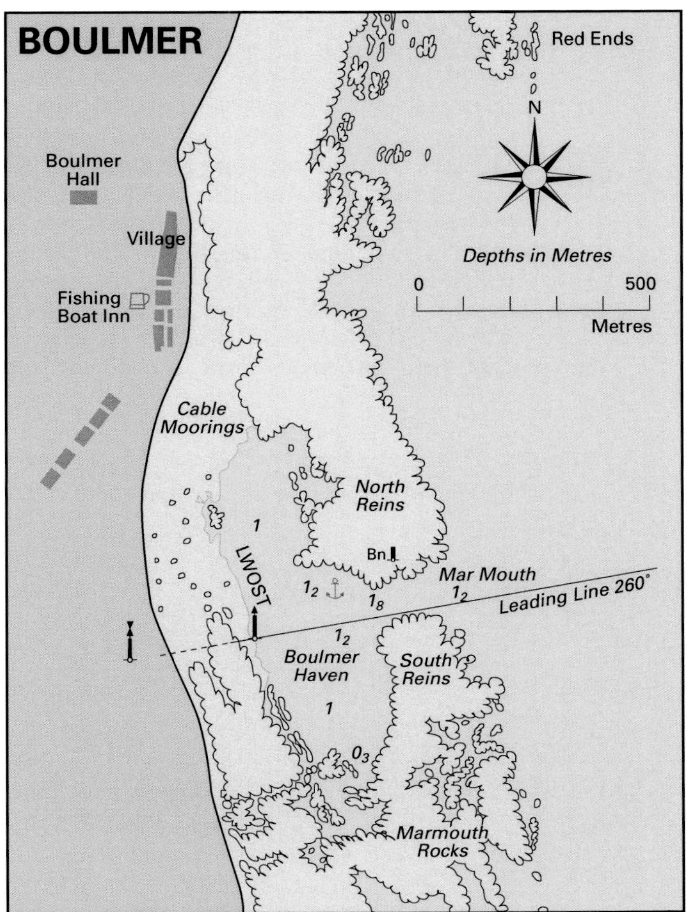

Entry is possible for a vessel drawing 1·5m only 1 hour. either side of HW and on very neap tides there may not even be sufficient water at HW. Once inside the estuary the best anchorage is obvious from the positions of the local boat moorings. These give easy beach access to the village, which is an extremely picturesque and delightfully concentrated Victorian resort. There are a couple of small hotels, three non-residential pubs, cafés, gift shops and a small general store but serious revictualling is not an option. Buses run hourly to Alnwick, the county town of Northumberland and the seat of the Percy family, the Dukes of Northumberland. This historic town is a must for the visitor to the county.

If Alnmouth is restricted to high water entry and exit, the next three anchorages provide a convenient complement by being most useful over the low water period. They are all nicely protected by girdles of rock, which provide perfect shelter except for two hours either side of HW, during which period any onshore weather will make for an uncomfortable roll. These circumstances can prove a boon to the northbound yachtsman who fancies a rest during the period of adverse tidal stream. The bulk of the S-going flood can be dodged neatly at any of these three delightful spots.

Boulmer

This little haven of clean sand is protected by crescent shaped reefs, which almost completely encircle it. This natural protection renders it unique among Northumberland anchorages in that it is tenable in weather from all directions though it would be unwise for the visitor to use the harbour in more than moderate onshore weather. When to this is added the bonus that it is possible in a limited area for craft drawing 1·5m to float at LWS then its utility and desirability become apparent.

It is not too easy to identify Boulmer haven from seaward though a mast associated with the RAF helicopter station

Approaches to Boulmer

gives approximate confirmation. From both N and S keep an offing of half a mile until the entrance can be identified, then approach directly from seaward. The most conspicuous entry feature is a beacon with a topmark at the S end of the North Reins reef. Behind this, on the beach, are the leading marks – two striped beacons with topmarks giving a leading line of 260° from which it is not wise to deviate owing to the narrowness of the entrance, the name of which is Mar Mouth. There is an alternative half tide entrance from the S out of Alnmouth Bay which is used by fishermen in heavy weather from north and east but this is not advisable without local knowledge or prior consultation.

There is a depth of 1·5–1·8m through the entrance channel and into the seaward part of the anchorage. It is best to anchor on or near the leading line as soon as the reef ends have been cleared. Craft drawing less, or willing to take the ground can proceed farther up the haven. To clear the western edge of the North Reins, keep on the entry line until the western gable of Boulmer Hall (a large conspicuous house) comes open W of the small pointed-roofed building on the foreshore. There are fishing boat moorings along this leading line and the visitor can anchor before or after them depending on draught and duration of visit.

Ashore there is a pub, a post office and a volunteer inshore rescue boat in the old lifeboat station, keeping alive a lifesaving tradition along this wild and rocky stretch of coast. This isolated haven was once notorious for smuggling and an evening spent before a roaring fire in the Fishing Boat Inn can be evocative. The pub is open all day.

Boulmer, pointed house

Boulmer *Airfotos*

Craster

Although sporting a small harbour, built for the shipping of the local whinstone, Craster is included in the 'anchorage' section because it dries out and because it becomes uncomfortable in heavy swell so that the visitor is just as likely to use it as an anchorage than as a harbour wall. Craster kippers are a watchword for excellence, stemming from the days when Scottish yawls used to land herrings in the season. The smokehouses still prosper though the herrings are brought in overland. The residual coble fleet is now concerned only with potting for crabs and lobsters.

The ruins of Dunstanburgh Castle, immortalised by Turner, provide a gaunt and unmistakable indicator to the approaches. One mile to the south is the harbour and anchorage, guarded by Little and Muckle Carr reefs, and entry can be made either side of the Little Carr, which has a stone beacon at its southern end. Between the Muckle Carr, which always shows, and the Little Carr beacon is a gap 40m wide with steep-to sides. Between the Little Carr and the mainland is another entry which has minimum depths of 3m LWS.

A good anchorage can be had in the spot where the two entry routes converge, just off the harbour entrance, and the Carrs afford protection from up to moderate swells. If a berth inside the harbour is required, entry can be made with a 1·5m draught 3 hours either side of HW and the best mooring is to be found against the east pier. The amount of water decreases slightly away from the harbour entrance and the bottom is of sand and pebbles overlying hard rock so mast rope precautions are wise. There are several wall ladders.

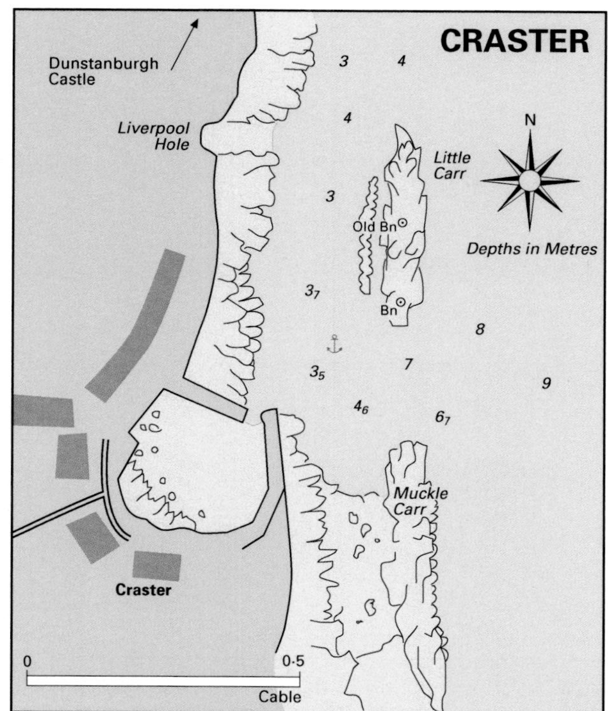

The famous kippers can be sampled ashore at a café attached to the smokehouse and there is a pub and a shop. One of the great attractions of a sojourn in Craster is the beautiful clifftop walk to Dunstanburgh Castle just over a mile to the north, perched on its natural rampart of the Whin Sill basalt.

Craster *Airfotos*

Craster and its approaches

Dunstanburgh and Craster

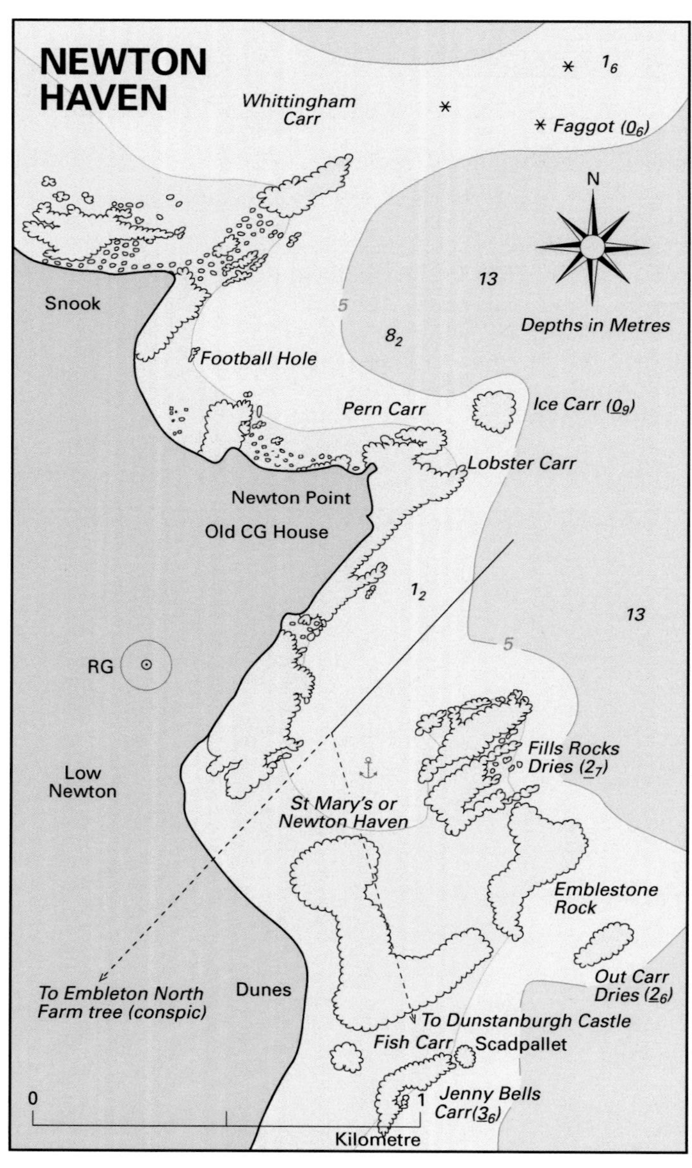

Newton Haven

This delightful anchorage is situated about the same distance N of Dunstanburgh Castle as Craster is to the S and affords a spectacular view of the ruin atop its basalt rampart. Its open-ended square of cream-washed cottages around a green behind the beach gives an aura of peace and tranquillity unmatched on the coast. This stretch is administered by the National Trust and is very popular with seabird and seal watchers. It offers good protection from winds from N by W to SSE and the offlying rocks serve to exclude residual swell from offshore.

The haven must be approached from the north by rounding Newton Rock buoy which marks the end of a series of rocks off Newton Point. From the south this same buoy must be approached to within half a mile before entering the anchorage. The most conspicuous feature of the approaches is an old CG watchhouse to the S of Newton Point. To clear the haven rocks from the S an approaching vessel must be seaward of a line from Bamburgh Castle through the isolated dry rock off Newton Point.

For the best water into the haven, align the first sand dune south of the village with the tree at Embleton North Farm. This line will pass close to the steep-to face of Fills Rock but there is room to err to the NW of the line. When Dunstanburgh Castle is in line with the most westerly hump of Emblestone Rock steer on that line which leads shortly and directly to the best anchorage. There are numerous local moorings inshore of this line but the line will be clear for anchoring and the best spot is as far south as possible given suitable depth

Sheltering girdle of rocks at Newton

soundings. There is a pleasant pub, the Ship Inn, ashore at Low Newton and another 0·75 miles away at High Newton. Both are open all day. There are no shops or other facilities, but the natural beauty is a sufficient lure in itself.

Beadnell

Beadnell Point, at the N end of Beadnell Bay, gives shelter to an anchorage in winds from N through W to SW. The ground is good sand but the presence of the Burn Carr rocks, just off the beach to the S, must be noted. Farther in, there is a tiny drying harbour surmounted by 18th century limekilns now owned by the National Trust. The harbour in fact faces west, so gives shelter in all but the most severe onshore conditions, but the lack of space and the presence of local cobles make an alongside mooring something of a problem. In an emergency, or even in less than an emergency, such as a desire to lean peacefully against a wall for the night, it is advisable to reconnoitre and ask locally before embarking on an entry. Bilge keelers can sit on the beach to the west of the harbour entrance.

There is little in the way of facility at the harbour and the presence of a nearby caravan site gives for seasonal congestion but a half mile walk to the village leads to two pub/hotels and a shop. Noteworthy is the Craster Arms which sports a grand coat of arms on the front wall and the remains of a medieval tower at the rear, still serving as a beer cellar for the pub. In northerly weather Beadnell can make an agreeable alternative to nearby Seahouses.

Newton-by-the-Sea *Airfotos*

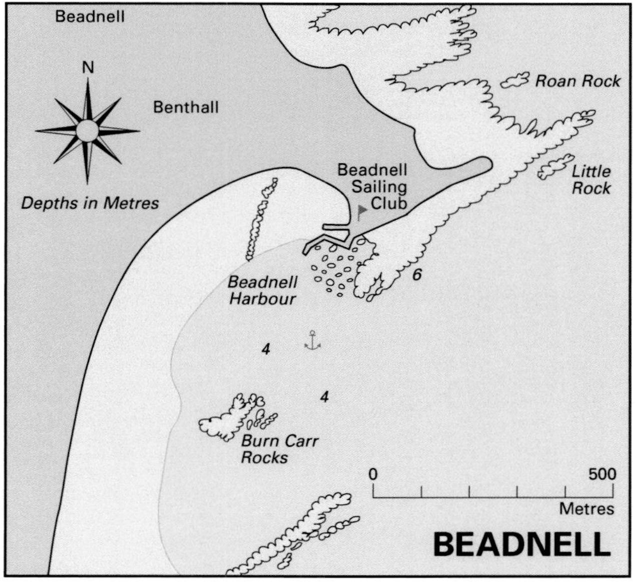

Beadnell *Airfotos*

Beadnell harbour

Beadnell – Polly standing in the harbour entrance

Seahouses

Seahouses is the fishing equivalent of a late 19th century mining village. Before this time the inland village of North Sunderland was a small agricultural community of no great note and the natural haven between two wedges of hard rock on the coast a mile to the east supported a few local beach and pot fishing familes who dwelt in a handful of poor cottages – the sea houses. The wealth of local fishing opportunities offshore, however, and the distance of suitable ports from which to exploit this wealth – Berwick to the N and Amble to the S – led to the creation of a harbour in the late 19th century. The shelter given by the natural rock shelves was reinforced by the building of piers and breakwaters as we see them today and a fishing community developed on a completely different scale to that which had previously existed. Terraces of fishermen's cottages stretched inland towards North Sunderland; shops, clubs, pubs and fishing services sprang up; a fleet of fishing boats of a much larger type than the local beach cobles worked the neighbouring waters for herring, whiting, cod and haddock.

The 20th century saw the development of a tourism that was becoming impatient of set piece Victorian and Edwardian resorts. People wanted to seek out nature and

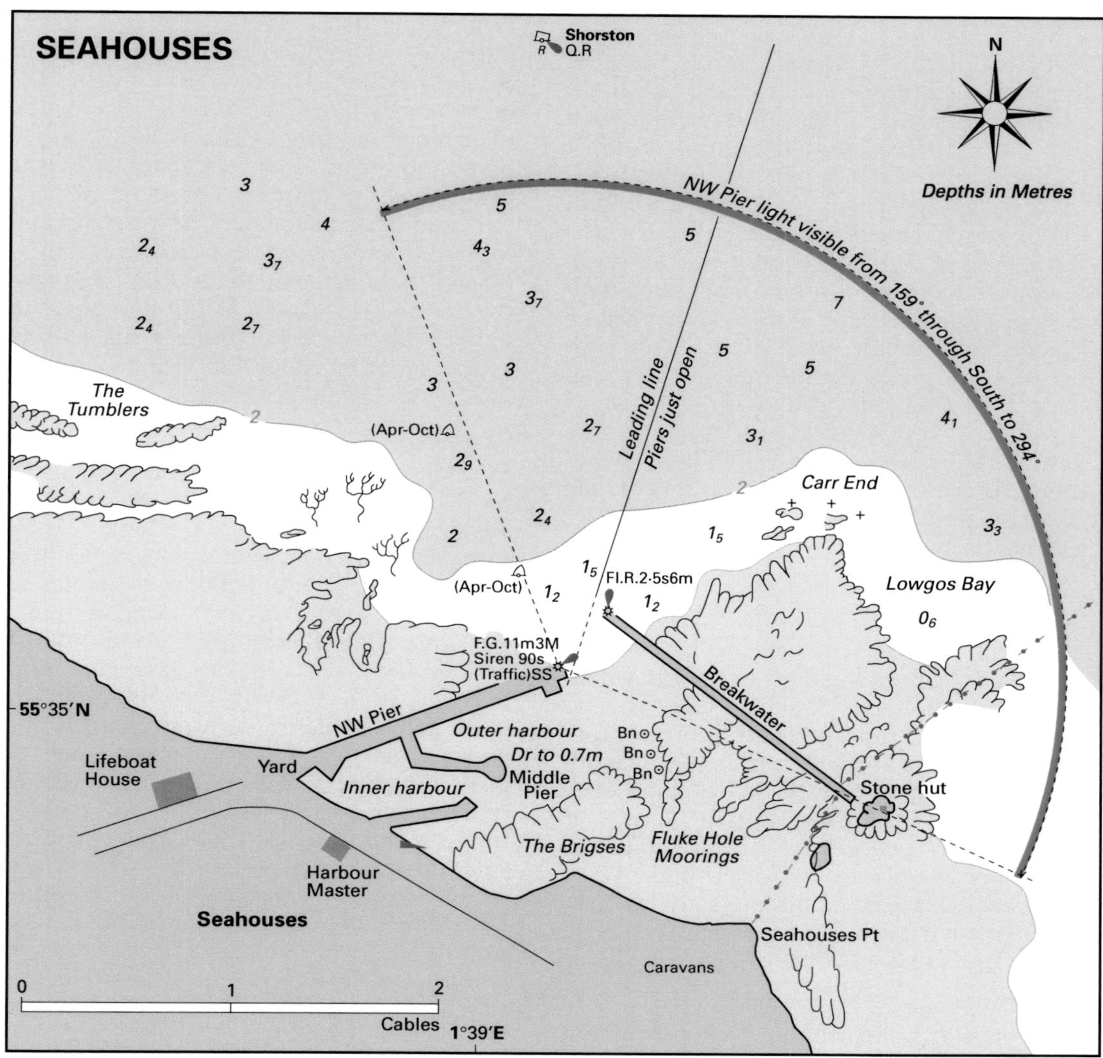

history and they travelled more widely in search of these things. The presence, near to Seahouses, of Bamburgh Castle on the one hand and the Farne Islands on the other, supplied history and nature in one neat little package. Seahouses became the centre for local boat trips to look at the rocks and bird life of the Farnes and it provided the service springboard for inspection of the historic wonders of Bamburgh some three miles to the north. In the way of 20th centry tourism such a role attracts seasonal wealth but also creates seasonal problems in the form of chip shops, candyfloss, knick-knack shops and crowded pubs. Local caravan sites provide accommodation for throngs of holidaymakers in peak season and at weekends out of season. Seahouses has its downside but its strategic utility renders it essential to pilotage considerations on the Northumberland coast.

Seahouses

Approaches

The Shorston Outcars buoy, situated between Seahouses harbour and the Inner Farne lighthouse, is crucial to the approach to the harbour. From the north a direct approach from the buoy leads between the pier ends. From the S the North Sunderland buoy should be left to port then steer on the Inner Farne lighthouse until the Shorston buoy is visible. Steer towards the buoy until the pier ends open, an approach can then be made. At night the fixed green sector light on the NW pier is visible from 159° through S to 294°. From the north, if this light can be seen, the beach rocks of Shorston are cleared. From the south the light serves merely to confirm the position of the harbour until the Fl.R(2·5) of the NE pier comes open of the green.

Entry

The harbour dries out at LWS and there is only half a metre or so of water between the pier ends. It is essentially a half tide harbour for craft drawing 1·5m though shoaler vessels have proportionately more time to operate. Indeed, small craft can be seen to-ing and fro-ing at LWN. The loading quay for the Farne Island trip boats is immediately inside around the end of the NW pier so beware of sudden traffic.

Inside the harbours attempts are made to dredge to a fairly uniform depth, though there is gradual shoaling towards the SW.

Moorings

The mooring situation at Seahouses is not always good. In quiet and offshore weather there is no problem, for the Outer Harbour is usually empty and a mooring can always be had on the NW pier. In onshore conditions, even moderate, a swell works into the Outer Harbour which makes for ranging and potential damage. It is untenable in stronger conditions. In such circumstances the Inner Harbour offers the only security but, Catch 22, this is when all the tripper and fishing boats come scuttling home and the place becomes congested. The harbourmaster must be consulted in such circumstances and it may be very difficult for him to arrive at a satisfactory solution.

Small local boats lie to moorings and take the bottom in Fluke Hole, but this is not an option for any vessel other than a bilge keeler. Harbour dues for visiting craft in 2015 were £10.00 per night, flat rate.

Facilities

In addition to the amusements, chips and candy floss already alluded to, the basics are all here, including a very large Co-op supermarket. Food, water, fuel, chandlery and engineering are handily available, as one would expect in a working harbour. Pubs are fine outside the hectic tourist periods and options for eating abound. One pub close to the harbour, The Olde Ship, is a truly remarkable repository of maritime paraphernalia, polished and presented in mind-boggling density. A working smokehouse has a retail outlet for smoked fish – a noted local delicacy. The visiting yachtsman will probably not opt for a trip to the Farnes – he may find it more rewarding and peaceful to run his own trip. A walk (or a bus) to Bamburgh, however, will lead to the impressive fortress that was the capital of the Northumbrian kings throughout the Saxon period, The castle was restored, and a trifle overdone by the Newcastle engineer Lord Armstrong in Victorian times but it is certainly worth a look and the village of Bamburgh is delightful.

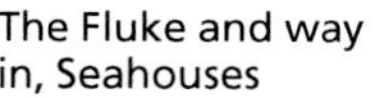

The Fluke and way in, Seahouses

Approaches to Seahouses

Seahouses entrance

Seahouses *Airfotos*

The Farne Islands

These Northumbrian islands have long exercised a fascination. The early Christian monks Aidan and Cuthbert, of whom more later, popped across the Sound with some regularity, presumably to escape the adoration of their putative disciples and indulge in peaceful communication with the Lord. The Farnes shot to prominence again in Victorian times. In 1838, Grace Darling, the twenty-three year old daughter of the keeper of the Longstone Light, peered out of her tiny bedroom window in the round wall of the lighthouse and saw the luxury steamer 'Forfarshire' aground on the Big Harcar rock half a mile to the west. She aroused her sleepy father and the pair of them rowed their little coble and rescued nine survivors in two trips. She became a celebrated heroine in the Victorian imagination even though she sadly died from consumption four years later.

The visitor to the Farnes today can still contemplate evidence of these things – St Cuthbert's chapel on Inner Farne and Grace's room in the Longstone lighthouse – but the magic of the Farnes for most people lies in the solitude and the bird life. An anchorage there, especially after the trip boats have returned to Seahouses, can be a wonderful experience.

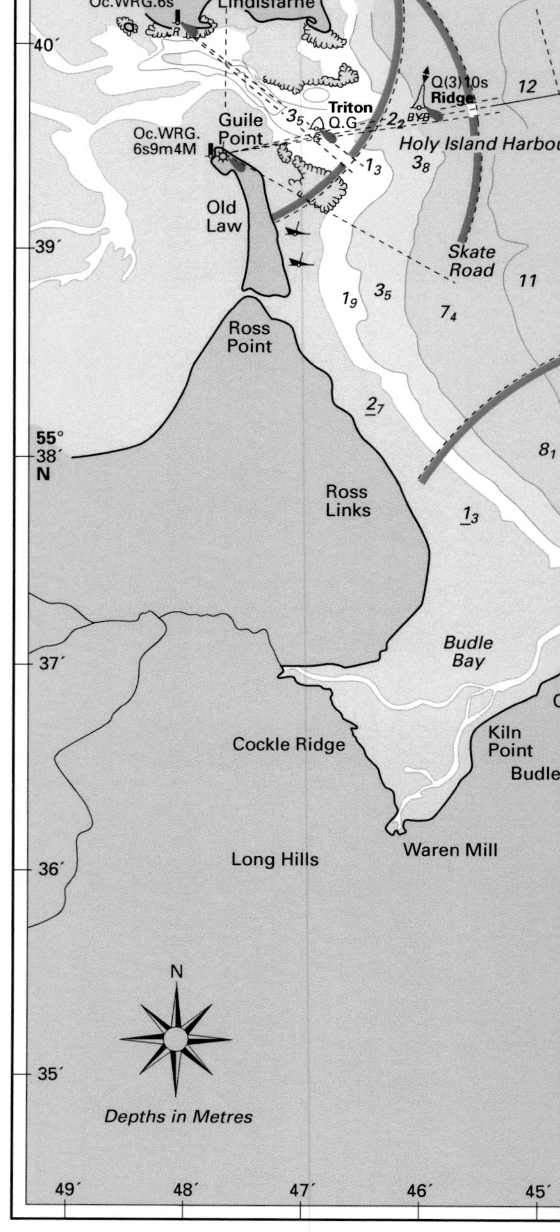

Farne Island Passages

The presence of the Farne Islands on a coastline otherwise fairly free of obstructions and prominent headlands has a marked effect on tidal streams. From being a fairly minor consideration they become an important ingredient of passage planning. The timing of the tidal streams follows the pattern of the coast in general with a 1·5 hour 'lag'. This means that the N-going ebb begins 1·5 hours after HW and the S-going flood 1·5 hours after LW. The rates vary according to the passage selected. The Inner Sound has a spring rate of 2·5 knots at full flow; Staple Sound has a 4 knot current and the Outside Passage up to 1 mile NE of the Longstone has 3·5–4 knots, decreasing rapidly seaward. Eddies develop where islets and rocks block or divert the stream, so great care must be exercised if indulging in close exploration and anchorage.

The Inner Sound

The North Sunderland and Shorston buoys mark mainland foul ground and must be left to port heading northwest. After passing the Inner Farne island group look out for the Swedman green conical buoy which must be left to starboard to avoid the Megstone. A strong wind against tide in the Sound creates considerable overfalls and these are best avoided by navigating close to the mainland beach.

At night the sectored Black Rock lighthouse at Bamburgh provides guidance through the Sound. From the south, steer on the Longstone Light until Black Rock changes from green to white then head for the Inner Farne light, also showing white. As the Inner Farne light is neared, and the island is clear right up to the cliff at this point, steer on Black Rock light, keeping in the white sector and keeping it bearing less than 280°. After 0·75 miles alter course to 300°; keeping in the white sector of Inner

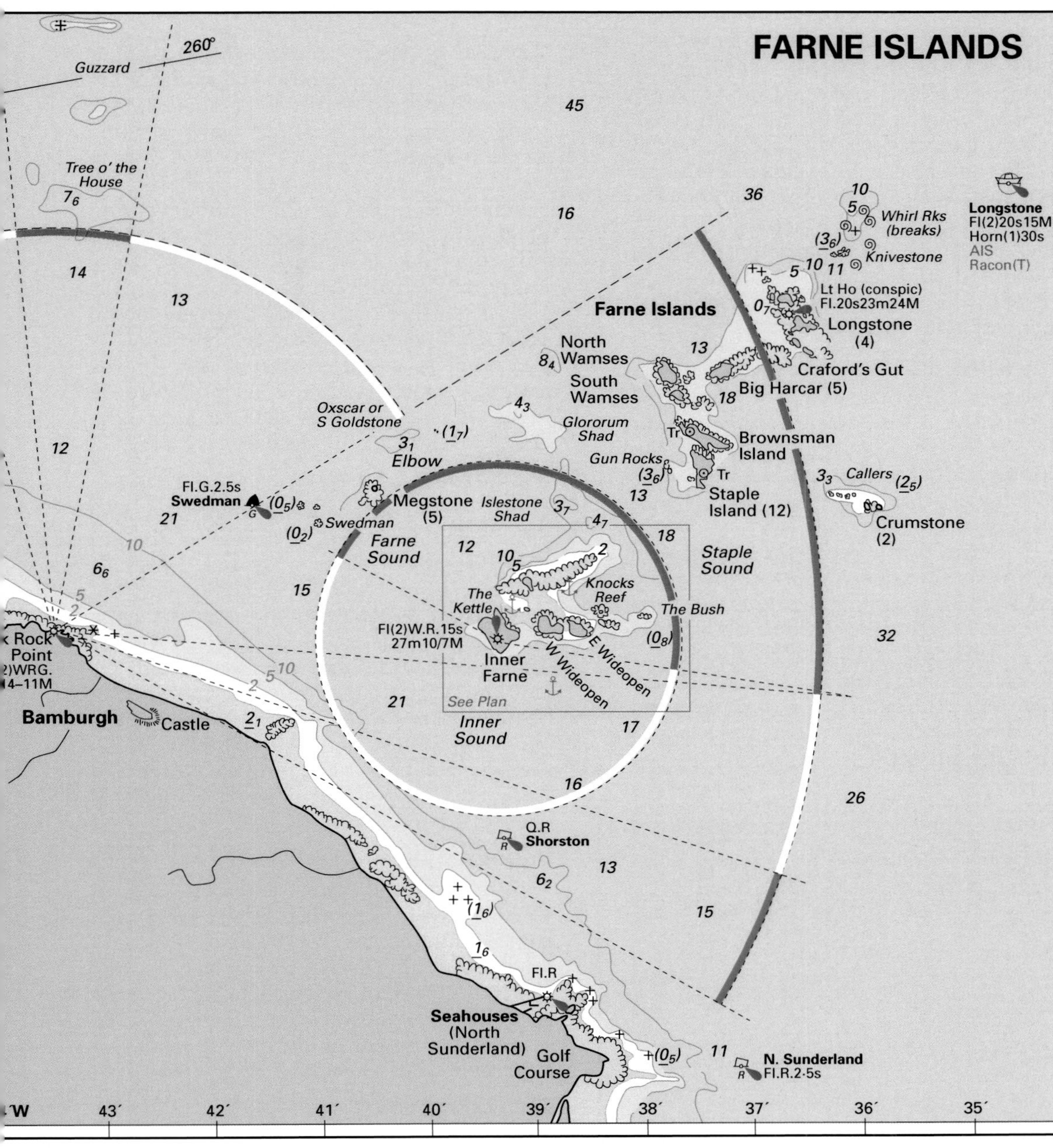

Farne, now aft of the beam, will ensure clearance of the Swedman buoy and the Megstone dangers.

From the north, steer on the Black Rock white sector until Inner Farne changes from red to white. Head roughly 125° to pass between 0·25 and 0·5 miles south of Inner Farne. Black Rock will change from white through red to white again and this sector should be followed to sea, keeping in the white sector of the Inner Farne. All this sounds complex but it is an extremely cleverly designed piece of sectoring and it gives navigational satisfaction without great risk.

The Staple Sound

This is an 0·5 mile wide passage between the Inner and Outer Farne island groups and it offers no advantages other than the very real one of experiencing the island scenery and its associated bird life at close hand. It is most often associated with seeking an anchorage. Staple Sound is not possible at night as the lighthouse sectors do not serve and its passage requires the use of transits.

The critical clearances on the SW side of the sound are the Bush, the Knocklin Ends and the Megstone. To the NE, the Crumstone, the Pinnacles of Staple Island and the Gun Rocks form a clearance line. From the SE, heading NW, a transit of the

Old Law beacons of Holy Island harbour with the Megstone clears the Bush but not quite the Knocklin Ends. Adjustment must be made for this piece of natural misfortune. Steering close to the Megstone will avoid the Oxscar danger. From the NW, heading SE, it is advisable to use the N side of the Sound as keeping the Crumstone clear of the Pinnacles gives clear water. All this is very exciting, and it needs no emphasis that the passage should only be attempted in good visibility, in no more than moderate weather and with a favourable tide.

The Outer Passage

There is no real case for the cruising yachtsman to pass outside the Farnes unless he is in a tearing hurry, in a race or has as destination somewhere in Scotland north of Montrose. The islands are not to be thus contemptuously ignored.

If, however, these are the circumstances, or if severe weather or bad visibility render the Sound impossible, then it is necessary to give the Longstone lighthouse an offing of at least 1·5 miles, to avoid offlying rocks, overfalls or breaking seas. It is also advisable to take a favourable tide. A recently installed light float, the Longstone, gives the safe offing.

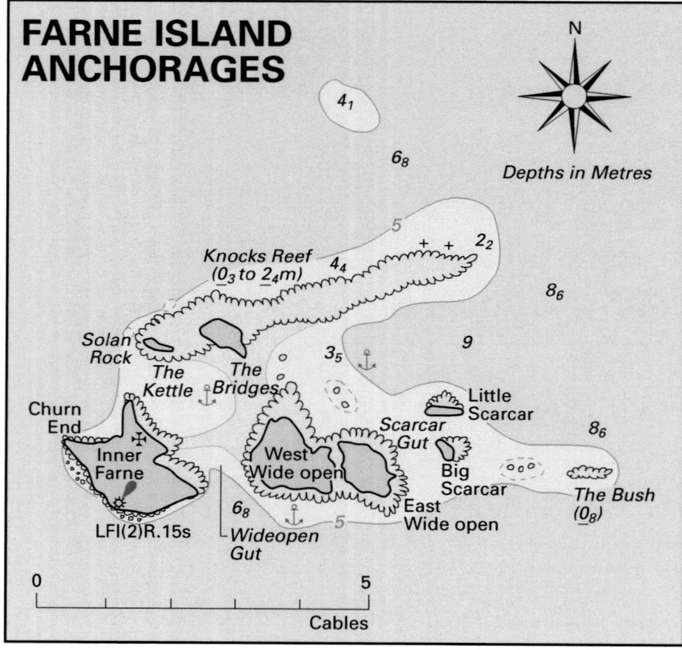

Farne Island Anchorages

The islands, about half of which cover at HW, are the seaward extension of the Whin Sill, an igneous intrusion responsible for some of Northumberland's most striking scenic features. Hadrian's Wall uses it as a natural rampart on which to build and the prominent castles at Dunstanburgh and Bamburgh surmount crags of it. Here, in the Farnes, it has been fragmented by wave attack and remains as a series of low rocks and islets. They are owned by the National Trust and landing is strictly controlled by the resident wardens, particularly in the nesting season. Landing is only allowed on Inner Farne, Staple Island and the Longstone and a landing charge is made.

The Kettle Anchorage

This lies immediately NE of Inner Farne and the main entry is north of the island and straightforward. Entry can also be made from the south through Wideopen Gut but only on the top half of the tide, the open period, of course, being determined by draught. The tide runs strongly through the Gut but in the Kettle itself an anchorage can be made out of the tidal stream, near to the tripper boat moorings. A dinghy landing at the jetty will enable the visitor to inspect St Cuthbert's chapel and there is a National Trust information centre.

Wideopen Anchorage

West Wideopen island is connected to Knock's Reef by a 'bridge' of sand and stones which covers at HW but not by very much. An alternative anchorage to the Kettle lies east of the bridge and is more sheltered in westerly winds. Entry is made from Staple Sound or through Scarcar Gut between the Scarcars and East Wideopen.

The Outer Islands

There are no good anchorages among the outer islands but in calm, clear weather they can be closely and rewardingly explored by boat to reveal a magnificent variety of seabird life. For detailed notes on exploration, the visiting yachtsman is advised to refer to the specialised Farne section of the RNYC Sailing Directions which do not date for the timeless Farnes.

Lindisfarne

Lindisfarne, or Holy Island as it is more popularly known, was the power house of the Celtic branch of early Christianity. In AD 634 King Oswald of Northumbria invited the saintly Aidan to come from Iona off the west coast of Scotland and establish a ministry there. This lasted for seventeen years until Aidan's death, when he was replaced by the reclusive Cuthbert. The king of the day, Eagfrith, somehow heard of him as he sat in his cell on Coquet Island and persuaded him, through the intermediary services of the abbess of Whitby, to become Prior and Bishop at Lindisfarne. Presumably the hustle and bustle of his new job proved too much for him and after two years he gave it up and retreated to Inner Farne where he died a year later. Given his rather thin track record as father to his flock it is rather surprising that he became such an icon to his followers, who carted his bones around the north of England for 100 years before finally depositing them in Durham Cathedral.

The Lindisfarne Priory was burned down by marauding Vikings in 875, but in the 11th century, when times were more peaceful, the Benedictine monks from Durham built another priory on the same spot, the ruins of which can be seen to this day. The Castle was built in the 16th century as part of a line of defences against the Scots, but Union followed so quickly that it was never really put to the test. As a consequence of this, and of some early 20th century restoration, it remains remarkably intact. These rich historical and mystical associations combined with the windswept natural beauty of the place make Lindisfarne a very popular place for visiting yachtsmen.

Approaches

From the south the visitor is likely to approach Lindisfarne by using the Inner Farne Passage (described previously). From the Swedman buoy at the N end of this passage steer on Emanuel Head at the NE corner of Lindisfarne, made conspicuous in daytime by its white triangular beacon. The Ridge End cardinal buoy at the harbour entrance will soon be identified, as will the Old Law beacons that give the initial entry alignment for the harbour.

From the north there are offlying rocks to be considered – the Plough Reef and the Goldstone. By day there is no problem passing between the island and the Plough W cardinal buoy but by night and in rough weather it is advisable to use the channel between the Plough and the Goldstone,

Old Law beacons – entrance to Lindisfarne

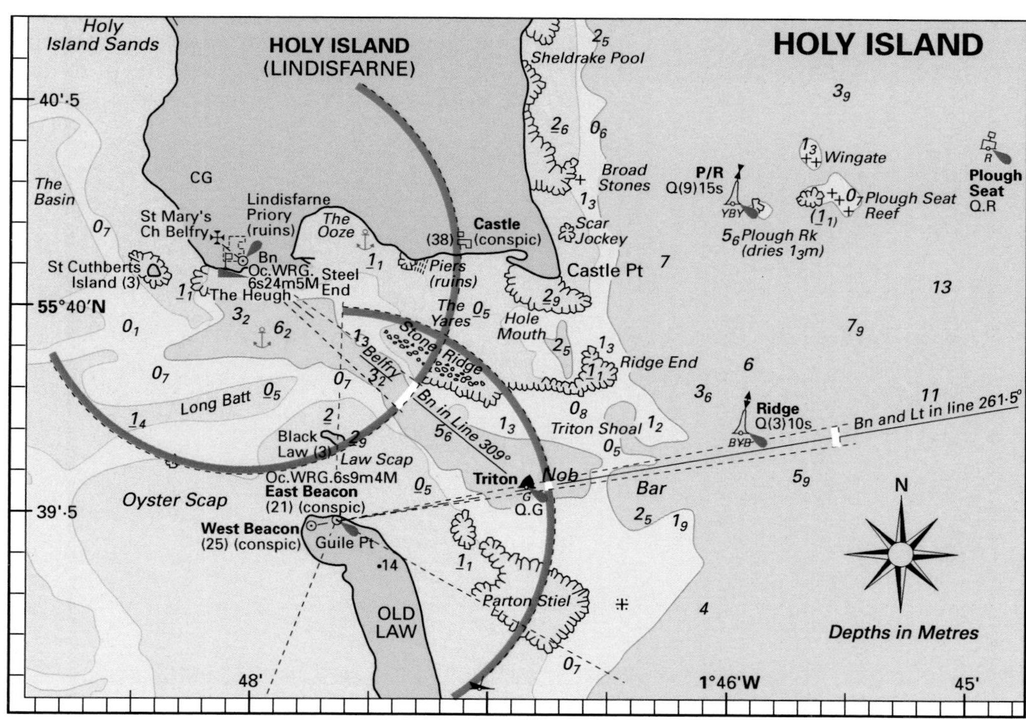

indicated by a red buoy to the E of the Plough and a green buoy to the W of the Goldstone. The white sector of Black Rock light guides through this channel at night.

Entry

From a point some 2 cables to the S of the Ridge End buoy the leading line can be easily followed along the line of the conspicuous Old Law Beacons (260°). At night the white sector of the light on the E Beacon leads along this line. After leaving the Triton green buoy to starboard the second leading line must be sought. Alter course when the transit of the large triangular beacon on the Heugh and the belfry of Holy Island Church is made. This leads directly into the anchorage. Once again the white sector of the light on the beacon gives guidance at night.

The harbour may be entered at all states of the tide by a craft drawing 1·5m but seas can break heavily on the bar in an onshore swell. In these circumstances it is advisable to wait for more water. The tide runs strongly – up to 4 knots at springs – so attention to timing is essential for a vessel with modest power. A more sheltered and tide-free approach can be made in the upper half of a tide through Hole Mouth and across the Yares (see chart).

Lindisfarne anchorage

Anchorage

The best anchorage is south of the Heugh in 3–6m. Local fishing boat moorings lie to the E of this, off Steel End, and some local yacht moorings are to the W, near St Cuthbert's Island. These mooring areas are best avoided. The tide runs strongly in the anchorage so care must be taken on the swing and whilst going ashore in the dinghy. If there is a strong W or SW wind over the high water period the anchorage can be uncomfortable.

Vessels able to take the bottom happily can dry out in sandy mud in the Ouse, a sheltered bay to the E of the Heugh. Here all the concerns of the anchorage can be laid to rest. The small jetty on Steel End is usually busy with the small boats of fishermen but in an emergency a yacht can dry out alongside it.

Facilities

There are several pubs and hotels in the village and all are geared up to dealing with tourists. Basic stores are available at the PO/grocery shop but there is no fuel on the island. A water tap stands on the village green. Lindisfarne mead is a local drink made from fermented honey. After a wedding the bride and groom were traditionally encouraged to quaff mead on every evening for a month, thus leading to the expression 'honeymoon'.

The real treat of a visit to Lindisfarne is simply to walk around, to breathe the air, look at the scenery, appreciate the birds and to wallow in its historic associations.

Lindisfarne *Airfotos*

Berwick upon Tweed

Historically suspended between England and Scotland, Berwick has excusably developed a split personality. Indeed, to this day the town is in England but its county is in Scotland. Its football team plays in a lowly division of the Scottish League and some historians maintain that it is still at war with Russia, having been forgotten as a party to a peace treaty centuries ago when English Parliamentary transactions did not include Berwick unless specifically mentioned. It changed hands no less than eleven times between 1174 and 1482. Queen Elizabeth I decided to put an end to all this nonsense and had constructed a modern defensive rampart featuring curtain walls and flanking bastions of the type later popularised in Europe by Vauban. There was a touch of the stable door about this gesture because shortly after completion there followed the Act of Union in 1603. The cessation of tussle can be seen as a happy sequel; another cause for celebration is that these magnificent ramparts, 1·5 miles in length, encircle Berwick to this day in a perfect state of preservation. In a magnificent piece of understatement Pevsner, the architectural historian, opines that Berwick 'is a town with a strong sense of enclosure'. Really?

In addition to the ramparts there are three noble bridges, the oldest built by James I in 1611 to celebrate Union and tie the knot, the most magnificent being the railway viaduct Border Bridge built by Robert Stephenson in 1847 and the newest, built in 1928, meriting no more comment than your average early 20th century bridge. Inside the ramparts there is a maze of streets and fine 18th century buildings which please the eye. Berwick is an undisputed gem of a place to visit and the surrounding scenery of coast and country make it a popular destination for the tourist (and yachtsman) of taste.

Approaches and entry

The mouth of the Tweed is easily recognizable from seaward and the approaches are clear of obstructions. A white lighthouse sits conspicuously on the end of the breakwater and the ramparts of the town rise majestically behind. A considerable amount of sand is constantly being moved around by the action of the river flow and the longshore drift so there is an unstable bar outside the line of the breakwater. In heavy weather from east or southeast a confused sea develops on the bar, exacerbated by the river ebb. In such circumstances entry should be avoided. In quieter conditions there is sufficient water at LWS for a vessel drawing 1·5m

Entry is best made parallel with the breakwater, approximately 10m south of it, and then head for a fairly conspicuous beacon (Q.G at night) beyond the western knuckle. Shortly after passing the knuckle, the Spittal leading marks will come into line on 207°. This lead must be followed as far as the second green conical starboard hand

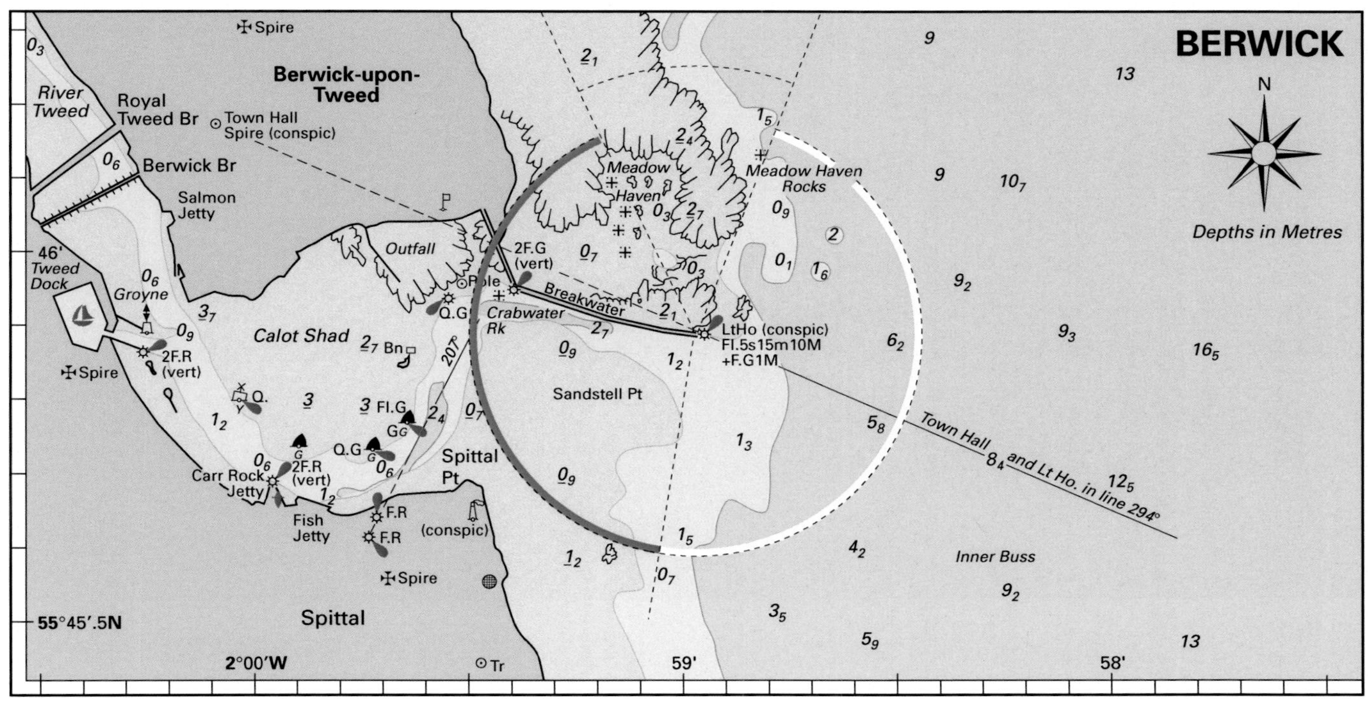

buoy whence a course can be steered for the Fish Jetty and on up to Tweed Dock. The green buoys are in shoal water so must not be passed too closely.

Mooring

The only real mooring possibilty in Berwick is Tweed Dock and it is advisable to contact the harbourmaster on approach (✆ 01289 307404, VHF Ch 12). If no response is received then a temporary mooring may be had at the western end of the Fish Jetty until contact is made. Tweed Dock no longer has gates so it is a tidal dock with a metre or so of water at LWS. The bottom is of soft mud so the slight grounding that may occur on big tides will scarcely be perceived.

The dock plays host to 2 or 3 coasters per week and several part time fishing boats but there is normally plenty of space for the visitor. Surprisingly, given the attractions of Berwick and the hinterland of Border towns, there has been no development of yacht facilities and there is only water to be had on the quayside. Overnight mooring fees in 2015 were £10 for craft up to 10m with small increments for larger vessels.

Facilities

The ambience of Tweed Dock is not overly prepossessing and the surrounding streets of Tweedmouth have a minimal array of shops and pubs. The Dock, however, is adjacent to Berwick Old Bridge and a short walk across will lead directly into the walled heart of the town. Here is a full range of shops, banks, churches, museums and pubs. A walk around the ramparts is a unique experience and will reveal a variety of historical and architectural treasures. Main line trains stop at the station and Edinburgh, Newcastle, York and London have direct services.

Berwick *Airfotos*

Eyemouth

The mouth of the Eye Water river has always afforded sufficient water and sufficient natural shelter to encourage port activity. Records from the 12th century show the commercial use of a simple riverside quay on the west bank and over the centuries piers were constructed to give more shelter to the entrance. In 1768 John Smeaton, the famous harbour and lighthouse engineer, constructed a great breakwater, sufficient to withstand any press of weather, and he developed the idea of diverting the course of the Eye Water so to reduce silting in his new basin. In this he was only partly successful, for the inner end of the basin gradually silted anyway. So in 1885 further harbour improvements introduced the sluices that we can see today, through which the flow of the Eye Water can, in a controlled manner, flush out any silt that accumulates in the inner basin.

Further devlopments to this unique harbour took place in 1964. Prior to this time, Smeaton's breakwater led across the present entrance from the eastern side and ended where the western pier head now lies. Entry was made by passing between the beach and this pier head. In 1964 the new eastern breakwater was led northwards, as we see it today, and the new entrance channel gave a more direct, if sometimes less placid, entrance.

Eyemouth is one of the more important of SE Scotland's fishing ports, with a large home based fleet of seiners and is frequently visited by fishing boats from other ports. In

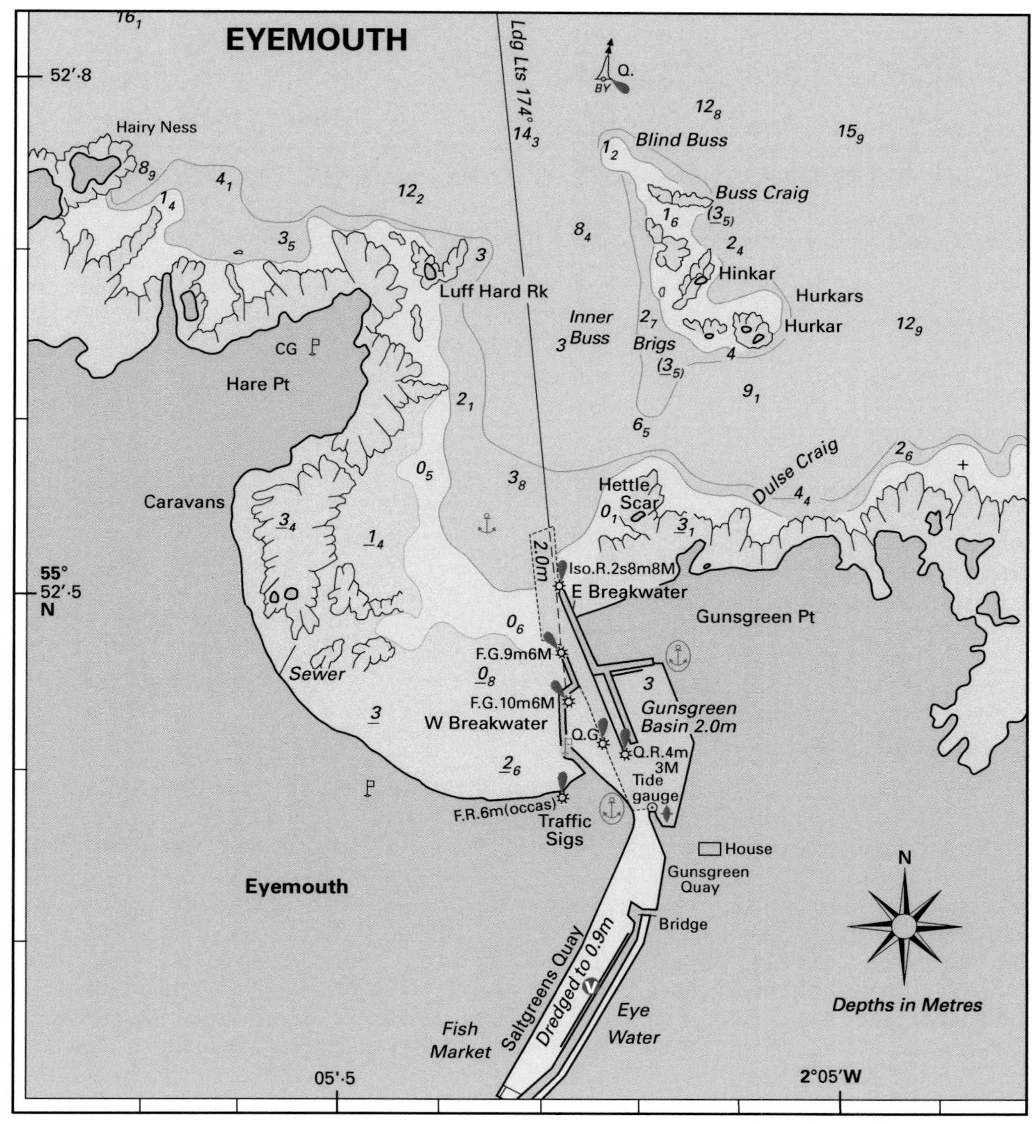

Eyemouth *Airfotos*

the late 1990s a new basin was dredged and constructed to the east of the entrance channel and a new fish market with landing facilities was constructed there. Fishing boats land here, and it is sporadically busy, but if the vessels are laid up for more than a day or two they are accommodated on the Saltgreens Quay on the west side of the inner basin. This quayside sports several impressive four storey granaries dating from the 18th century when there was a lively commerce in agricultural products. This has now gone and the fishing rules supreme.

Approaches and entry

Although fronted by a set of formidable rocks, the Hurkars, against which the seas heave and break, sometimes menacingly, the approaches to Eyemouth are quite clean and steep-to and the Hurkars are regarded as protective friend rather than foe. From the north a passage between Luff Hard rock, off Hare Point, and the offlying Hurkars will bring leading marks into view on a course of 174°. These are orange posts on the west pier (F.G. at night) and the line leads close to the light on the end of the E breakwater.

From the south, there are no leading marks, but a course to pass midway between the Hurkars and Hettle Scar, off Gunsgreen Point, will give deep water. As soon as the piers open, turn south for the harbour entrance on the leading marks as described above. Heavy winds from the north to east render the approaches and entrance unsafe. In these circumstances a red flag by day or a FR light by night indicate that the harbour is closed.

A vessel drawing 1·5m may enter the harbour at any state of any tide for the entrance is dredged to 2m LAT. Inside the harbour, the new Fish Basin to the east has 3m LAT and the Inner Basin has 1m LAT. After passing fairly close to the E pier end, keep slightly to E of centre for the best water. The entrance channel or 'canyon' as it is sometimes called is only 16m wide so vigilance must be maintained for fishing boat movements.

Moorings

Visitors are welcome but because Eyemouth is a busy fishing harbour mooring instructions must always be taken. The harbourmaster (✆ 01890 750223, VHF Ch 12) is on duty from 0700 until 2000 and will direct as necessary. In the event of non-contact or if arrival is made in the 'quiet hours' then a temporary mooring can be had at the southern end of the new Fish Basin on the east side.

In 2015 the visitor rates were £20.30 (incl. VAT) per day up to 10m, increasing incrementally.

Facilities

The new Fish Market is well endowed with facilities and visitors are welcome to use them. Showers and toilets are available in the market complex, and fresh water and power points occur all along the quays. Fuel and repair facilties are present in a way commensurate with a busy near water fishing port.

Farther ashore, the town facilities are adjacent to the Saltgreens Quay, pubs, shops and restaurants will serve the requirements of all but the most demanding visitor. The quayside taverns still reverberate with what passes in the 21st century for nautical swagger so an amusing evening is guaranteed. In the old Georgian church is a museum commemorating the Eyemouth Fishing Disaster of 1881 when 189 local men lost their lives. This serves to chillingly remind the cruising yachtsman of what can happen when a cruel sea strikes an iron bound coast.

Small Berwickshire harbours

In offshore or settled weather conditions there are two small harbours in the vicinity of Eyemouth which the visiting yachtsman may want to profitably investigate. This profit will derive not from facilities, which are minimal compared with what Eyemouth has to offer, but from the beauties of nature. The tortured, folded Silurian rocks have been eroded to provide some of the finest cliff scenery in Britain, with off-lying stacks that provide home to a spectacular quantity and variety of sea bird life. The auk family – puffins, guillemots and razorbills – are well represented, and among them can be seen elegant kittiwakes, spitting fulmars and bullying skuas. These little harbours are a treat in decent weather.

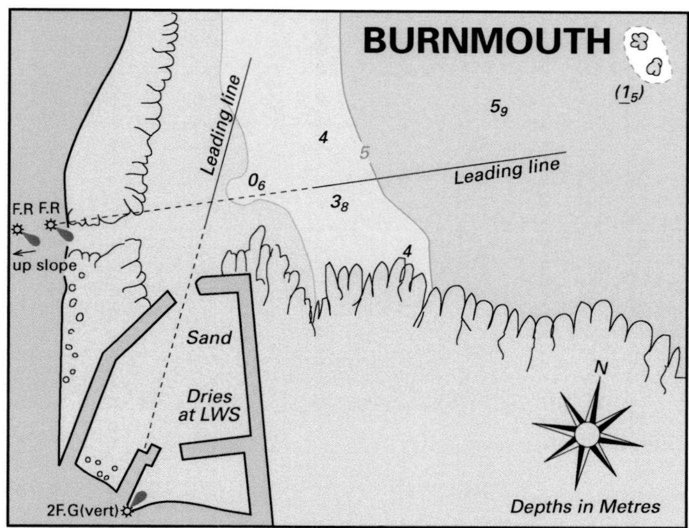

Burnmouth

Two and a half miles south of Eyemouth, Burnmouth can be easily identified from seaward by its dramatic ravine, at the foot of which are terraces of fishermen's cottages. From land, especially from the train, it requires a great deal more vigilance to identify it. The east coast main line emerges from a deep cutting only to plunge into another one twenty yards farther on. This break in the cuttings is where the train bridges the Burnmouth ravine, and the alert passenger, with nose glued to the eastern window of the train, will catch a momentary glimpse of a truly spectacular sight. There, at the foot of the ravine, lies a wondrous little rock-girt harbour, surrounded by fishermen's cottages.

The approach from sea involves sailing WSW on leading marks immediately north of a row of white cottages well above the shore line. These marks are white painted and carry red lights at night, though this must be seen as a guide to local fishermen

Burnmouth from N
Airfotos

Burnmouth's canyon

rather than as siren to the nocturnal yachtsman. This line should be followed until the harbour entrance opens and then direct entry can be made, the time limits for 1·5m draught being 4 hours either side of HW.

Before 1830, local fishermen simply used the natural rock protection and fished off the beach, but the stout walls built to give additional protection still stand to this day. The best water is against the east breakwater but the harbour dries completely on the biggest of springs so vessels will have to be prepared to take the bottom in these circumstances. At neap tides a vessel drawing 1·5m will just about remain afloat.

It is a pleasant, if steep, walk up the ravine to the main A1 road where there is a pub and a small local shop.

St Abbs

Two miles north of Eyemouth, St Abbs is another breathtakingly attractive little harbour. It faces NNW so a vessel approaching from the south must round the numerous offlying rocks which front the village to a distance of 0·25 miles. The conspicuous Maw Carr rock, reddish in colour and 15m high stands 120m N of the harbour entrance. Steer to pass close to seaward of the Maw Carr – close enough for the harbour entrance to open to the south. This approach seems not for the faint of heart but in fact the dangers are all visible and nothing nasty lurks beneath the surface, provided the directions are reasonably followed. The Hog's Nose covers at HWS and a transit of the south face of the Maw Carr and the reddish village hall on the cliff north of the village will clear it.

From close to the Maw Carr a leading line can be followed (yellow pole on centre quay in line with lamppost on south quay, both FR at night) but in fact any direct route from the Maw Carr to the open entrance will have good water at all but LWS. Berthing will depend on the situation with the local inshore fishing boats, but the best area is the southern end of the east wall. There is rather more depth than in Burnmouth and the harbour always has water but a craft drawing 1·5m will touch the bottom on LWS.

Water and toilets are available and there is a pub half a mile inland but the essence of a visit to St Abbs is to drink in scenery rather than heavy, fizzy Scotch bitter. There are fine coastal walks in both directions and St Abb's Head, a mile and a half to the north, is particularly recommended for its cliff scenery and bird life.

St Abbs approaches *(above)* and St Abb's Head from S *(below)*

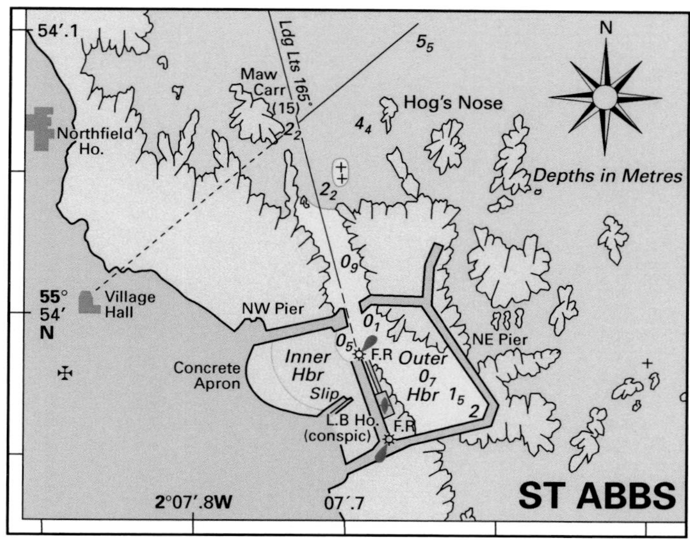

St Abbs harbour *(top)* and St Abb's Head from N *(above)*

St Abbs *Airfotos*

Northern Departures

(see Imray C 27 Firth of Forth)

Only a dedicated flat-earther would turn round at St Abbs and retreat to the south simply because the pilot book runs out here. Just around the corner is the Firth of Forth, one of Britain's finest cruising grounds. There are so many harbours that a yachtsman could count himself unlucky if he shut his eyes, aimed for the coast and did not end up in one. Many of them are tidally restricted but they are almost invariably interesting and unique. It is almost inconceivable that sailing plans could be totally thwarted by weather for there is always somewhere to point. The pilotage for this cruising ground is laid out in great detail by Nicholas Thompson in the Forth Yacht Clubs' *Pilot Handbook*. Suffice it to note here that there are a number of all-tide harbours in which shelter can be sought. On the south side are Dunbar, Leith, Granton and Port Edgar. On the northern, or Fife, coast Inverkeithing, Burntisland, Methil and Pittenweem all offer low water access and shelter to a craft drawing 1·5m. Some of these places are rough; some may be less than welcoming; but in a crisis, anything will do. The Firth of Forth is a fine cruising ground.

Distances and tidal information

	Distance from Spurn Head (sea miles)	*HW time differences on Tees entrance (in minutes)*	*Rise of Tide (m) Springs*	*Neaps*
Bridlington	35	+0060(S) +0050 (N)	5	2·4
Scarborough	51	+0040	4·6	2·3
Whitby	67	+0014	4·8	2·3
Hartlepool	90	_0010	4·3	2·2
Seaham	100	_0015	4·5	2·1
Sunderland	105	_0017	4·6	2·2
North Shields		_0017	4·3	2·1
Blyth	119	_0032(S) _0020(N)	4·2	2·2
Amble	134	_0035(S) _0028(N)	4·2	2·1
North Sunderland		_0110(S) _0106(N)	4·1	2·1
Holy Island	155	_0110(S) _0106(N)	4·2	2·2
Berwick	168	_0120	4·1	2·5
Eyemouth		_0120	3·9	1·6
St Abbs	172			

Tidal streams

The figures against the arrows denote mean rates in tenths of a knot at neaps and spring. Thus 06, 11 indicates a mean neap rate of 0·6 knots and a mean spring rate of 1·1 knots.

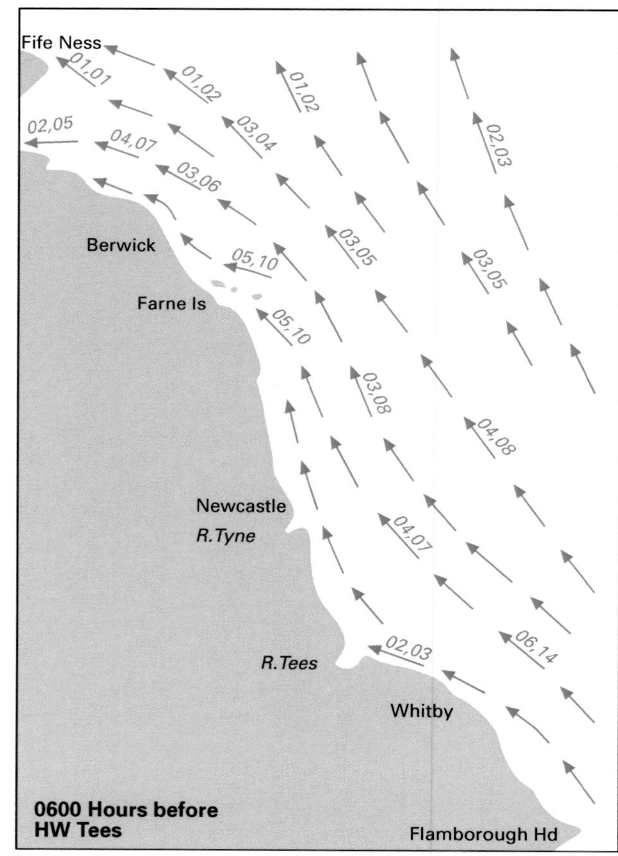

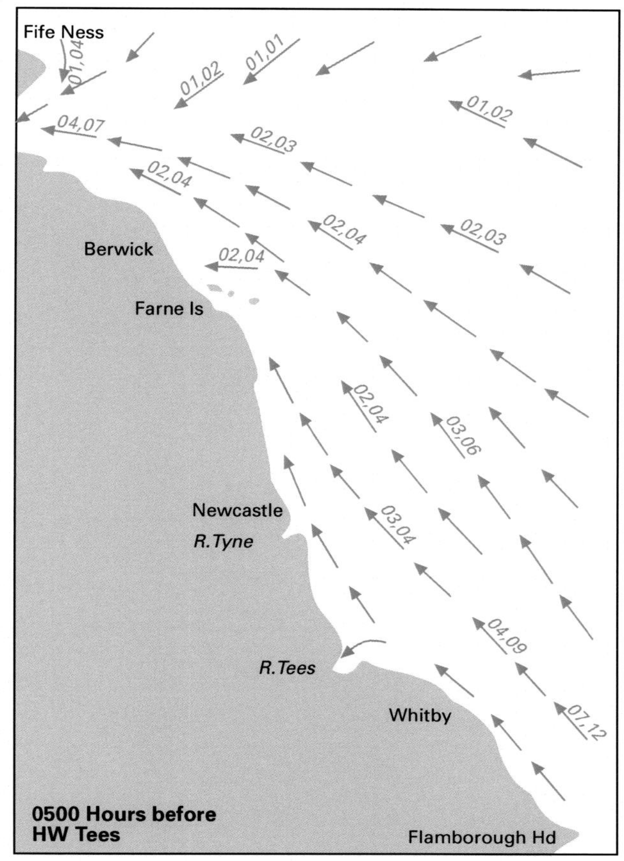

0500 Hours before HW Tees

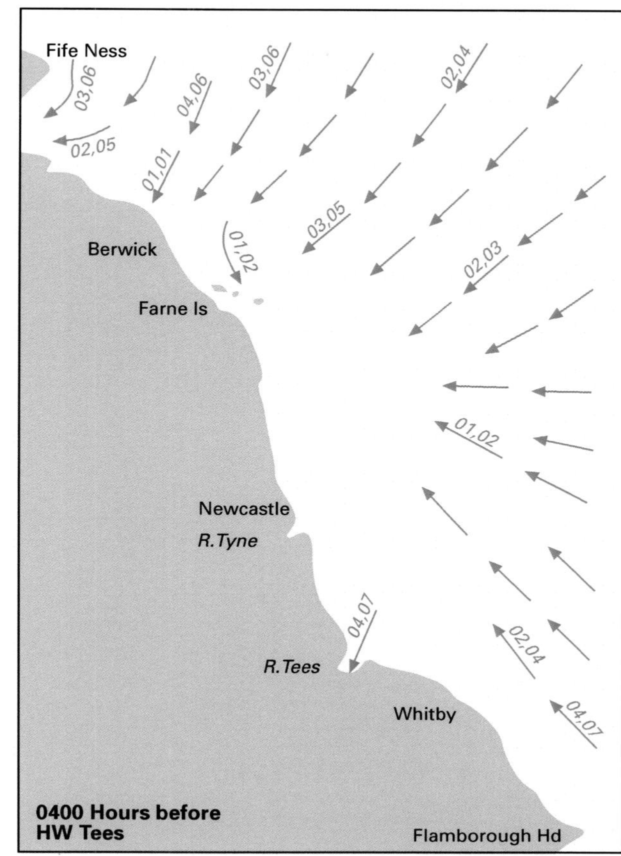

0400 Hours before HW Tees

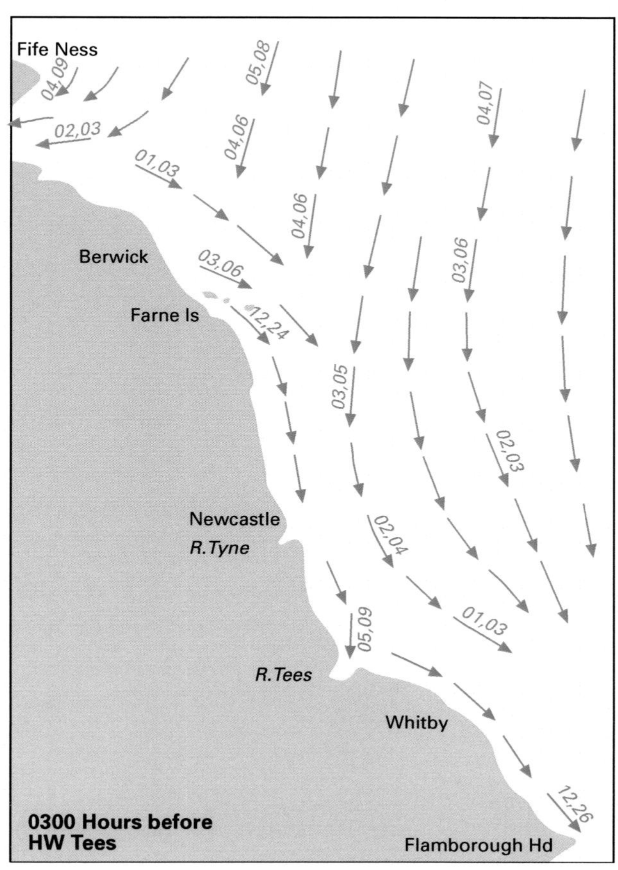

0300 Hours before HW Tees

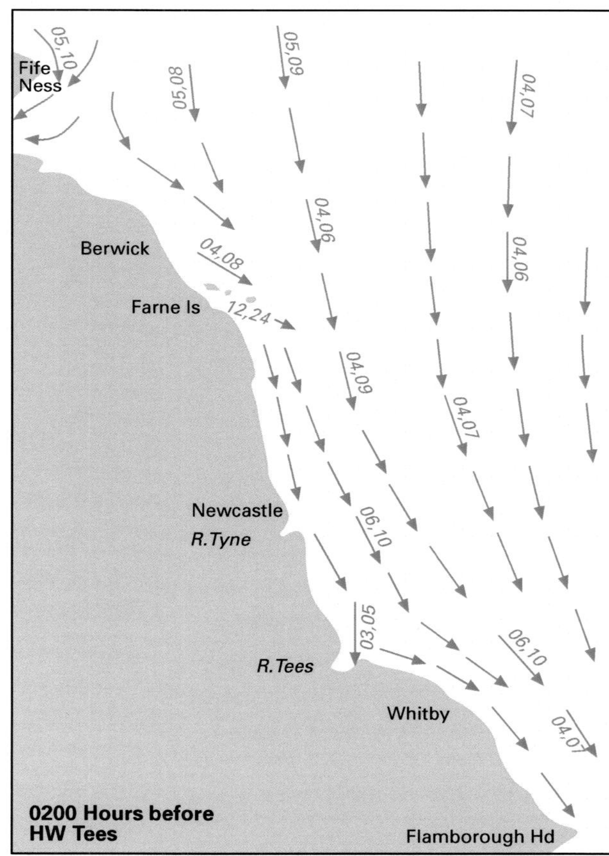

0200 Hours before HW Tees

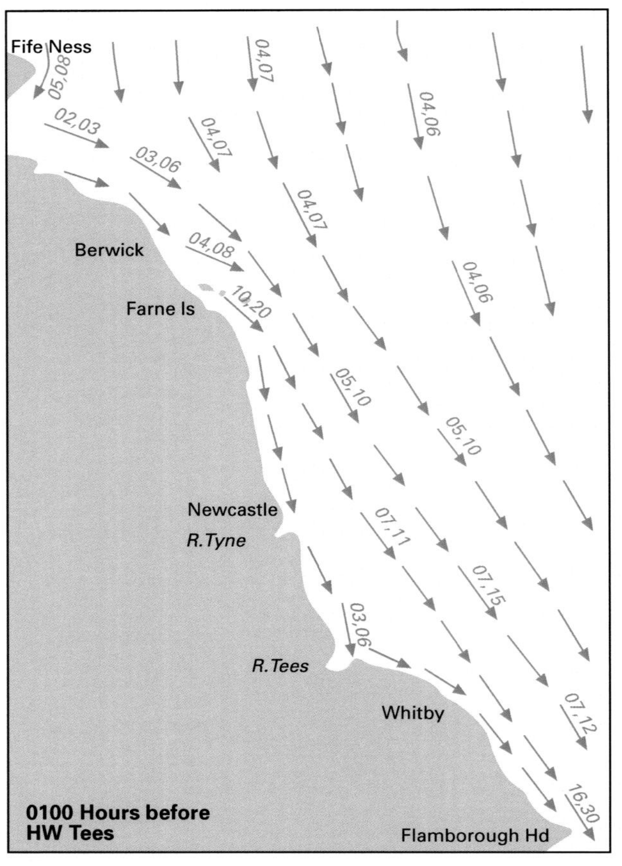
Fife Ness
05,08
04,07
04,06
02,03
03,06
04,07
04,07
Berwick
04,08
Farne Is
10,20
04,06
05,10
05,10
Newcastle
R.Tyne
07,11
07,15
03,06
R.Tees
Whitby
07,12
16,30
0100 Hours before
HW Tees
Flamborough Hd

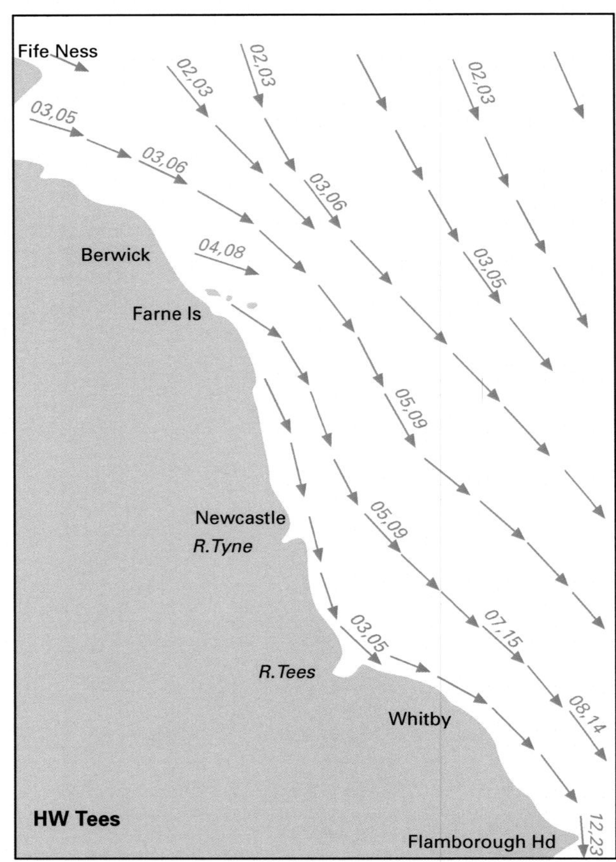
Fife Ness
02,03
02,03
02,03
03,05
03,06
03,06
03,05
Berwick
04,08
Farne Is
05,09
Newcastle
R.Tyne
05,09
07,15
03,05
R.Tees
08,14
Whitby
HW Tees
Flamborough Hd
12,23

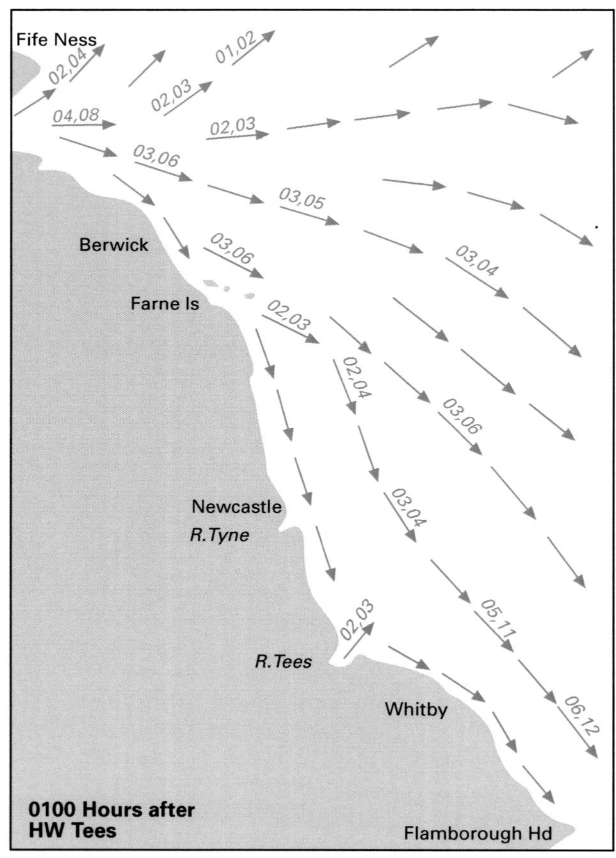
Fife Ness
02,04
01,02
02,03
04,08
02,03
03,06
03,05
Berwick
03,06
03,04
Farne Is
02,03
02,04
03,06
Newcastle
R.Tyne
03,04
05,11
02,03
R.Tees
Whitby
06,12
0100 Hours after
HW Tees
Flamborough Hd

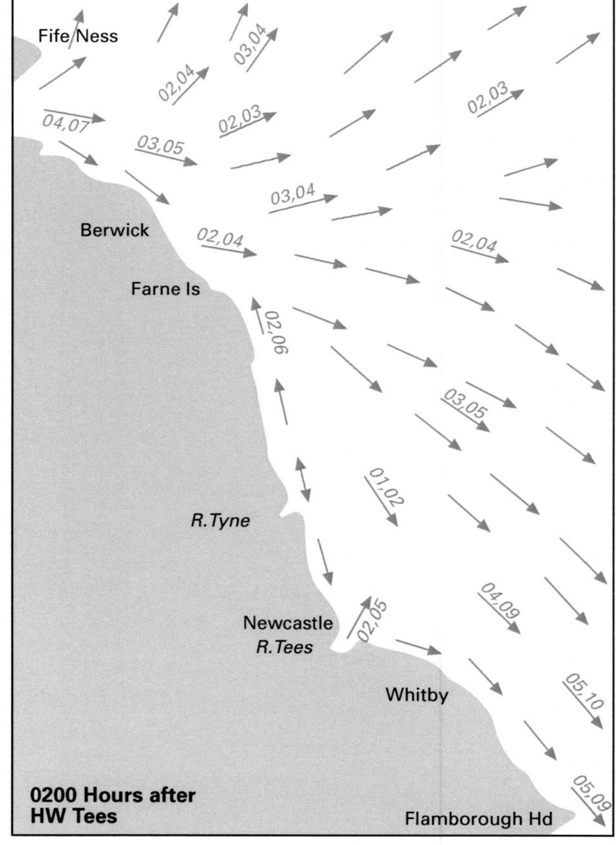
Fife Ness
03,04
02,04
04,07
02,03
02,03
03,05
03,04
Berwick
02,04
02,04
Farne Is
02,06
03,05
01,02
R.Tyne
04,09
Newcastle
R.Tees
02,05
Whitby
05,10
05,09
0200 Hours after
HW Tees
Flamborough Hd

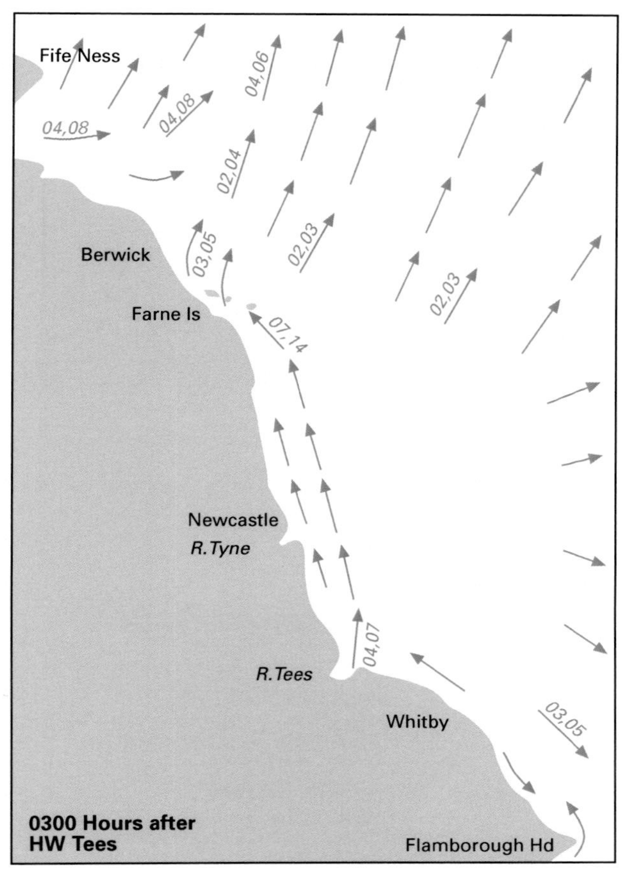
Fife Ness
04,08
04,08
04,06
02,04
Berwick
03,05
02,03
02,03
Farne Is
07,14
Newcastle
R.Tyne
04,07
R.Tees
Whitby
03,05
0300 Hours after
HW Tees
Flamborough Hd

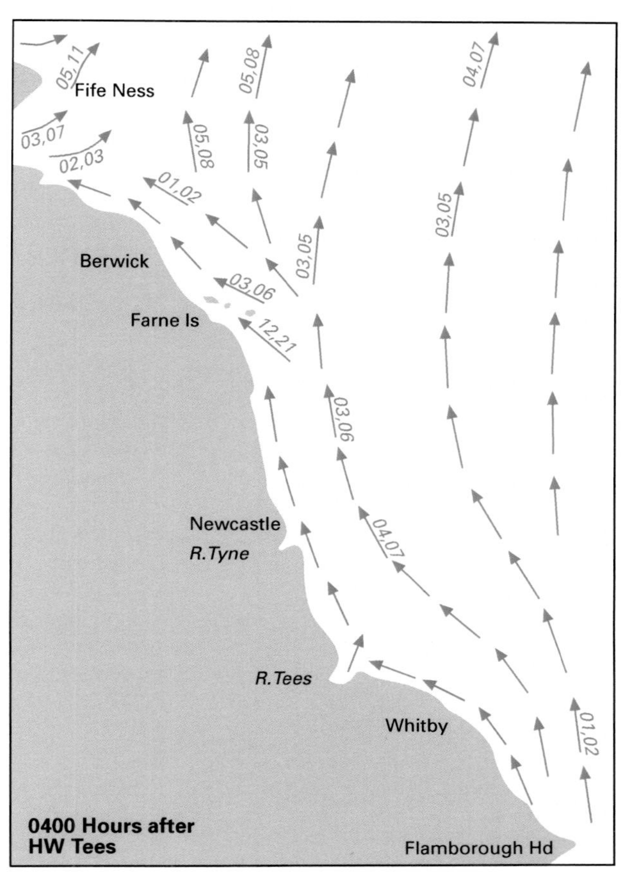
05,11
Fife Ness
05,08
04,07
03,07
02,03
05,08
03,05
01,02
Berwick
03,05
03,05
03,06
Farne Is
12,21
03,06
Newcastle
R.Tyne
04,07
R.Tees
Whitby
01,02
0400 Hours after
HW Tees
Flamborough Hd

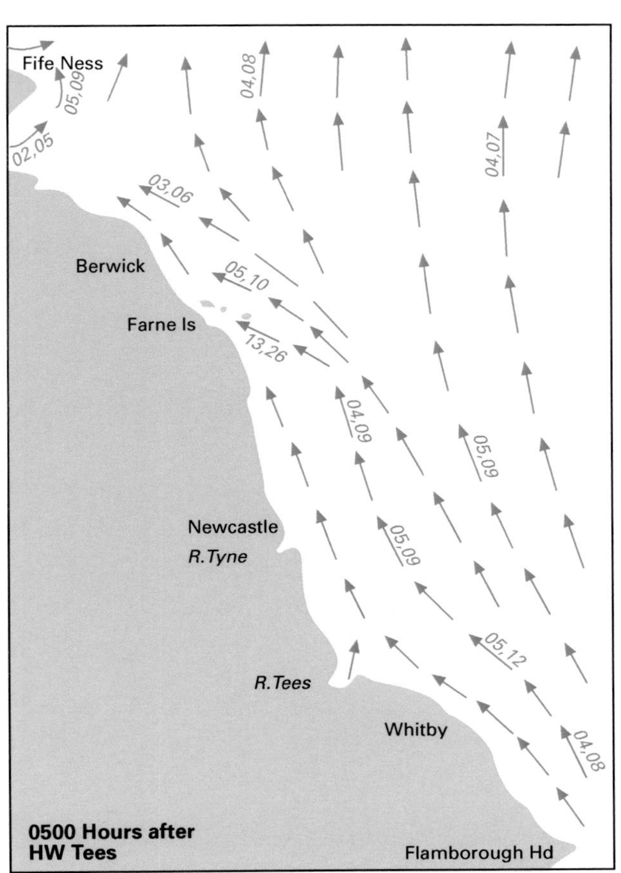
Fife Ness
05,09
04,08
02,05
04,07
03,06
Berwick
05,10
Farne Is
13,26
04,09
05,09
Newcastle
R.Tyne
05,09
05,12
R.Tees
Whitby
04,08
0500 Hours after
HW Tees
Flamborough Hd

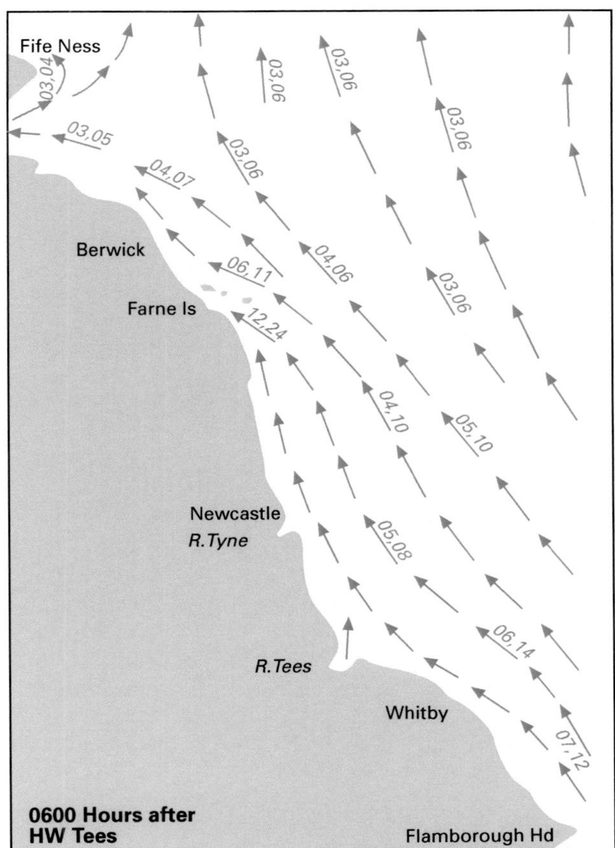
Fife Ness
03,04
03,06
03,06
03,05
03,06
04,07
03,06
Berwick
06,11
04,06
03,06
Farne Is
12,24
04,10
05,10
Newcastle
R.Tyne
05,08
06,14
R.Tees
Whitby
07,12
0600 Hours after
HW Tees
Flamborough Hd

Index